IN THE BALANCE

THE HORSEMAN'S GUIDE TO LEGAL ISSUES

By George G. Johnson, Jr.,
Attorney at Law

Published by Pica Publishing, Golden, Colorado, U.S.A.

Warning - Disclaimer

This book is designed to provide information in regard to the subject matter covered. It is sold with the understanding that the publisher and the author are not rendering legal or professional services herein. Federal and state laws are constantly changing, and no single book can address all legal situations.

Printed and bound in the United States of America

Cover design by Brigitte Nadon

Johnson, George G.

In the balance : the horseman's guide to legal issues / George G. Johnson, Jr.

p. cm.

Includes index.

ISBN 0-9630558-0-1

1. Horse industry--United States--Law and legislation. I. Title.

HD9434.U52J64 1993 338.1'761'026

QBI93-624

DEDICATION

To my wife, Beth, and my sons, Pete and Andy

About the Author

George G. Johnson, Jr.

George G. Johnson, Jr., shares his years of experience and knowledge of equine law with readers inside these pages. The wide range of topics helps everyone in the horse industry. From a beginner purchasing their first horse, learning what paperwork is involved in a purchasing agreement to buying horse property. People who are well into the horse business will want to clearly understand the "two of seven presumption," as the IRS sees it. While state horse councils are working on everything from workmen's compensation to limiting the liability of horseowners - find out what you are responsible for now. Of course there is a chapter on contracts, however there are no forms to use, since this only complicates matters in different situations and states.

George G. Johnson, Jr., is the author of several national magazine articles regarding equine law, covering subjects like: *Horseman's Liability, Equine Law: Handshake and a Written Agreement, Equine Law: Colorado Has New Limits on Liability for Horse Activities, Remember Your Horse in Your Will.*

Johnson has served as a member and president of the Denver Agricultural and Livestock Club and has been active as a volunteer coordinator for the Denver National Western Stock Show. He also guest lectures at Colorado State University regarding equine law. Other related activities include being a member and past president of the Denver Dumb Friends League Animal Shelter.

Since being admitted to the bar in 1965, he has written several other published works and served on many committees, too numerous to mention.

Johnson is currently licensed to practice law in both Colorado and Texas.

Table of Contents

Table of Cases

Foreword

Horses can be a great source of pleasure to men and women living in today's complicated world. Horses can also become a serious threat to our peace of mind and physical health if we are unaware of the inherent risks in equine activities. Ignorance of laws relating to horses can also place our wealth, as well as our happiness in jeopardy.

This book contains current legal advice on our responsibilities and risks in owning and caring for horses. In addition, there is extensive information on the business of owning and managing a horse enterprise. I am impressed with the breadth and depth of the information presented. The text is written in layman terms and contains a glossary of legal terms with application to horse-related issues.

This book and future updated editions would be a valuable reference in every horseman's library. Hopefully, potential horse owners will obtain and read the book before they purchase a horse. Unfortunately, the element of accountability of one's own actions has almost been forgotten in American law.

This text will be especially valuable to the students in my Equine Production and Industry class at Colorado State University. Mr. Johnson's lecture is a popular part of our class because of his unique "common sense" way of relating the legal profession to the equine industry.

Mr. Johnson consistently emphasizes the need for careful planning to prevent problems. "Remember, the best law is preventative law," and "Get it in writing" frequently appear throughout the book. Studying this book should be every horseman's first step in preventative law.

Doug Butler, PhD, FWCF
Associate Professor
and Equine Science
Teaching Coordinator
Colorado State University

* FWCF stands for the Fellowship of Worshipful Company of Farriers. Dr. Butler is one of only 50 people in the world who have achieved this title by passing written, oral and practical exams. Dr. Butler is the first person outside of the United Kingdom to have earned this title.

Chapter 1

Forms of Equine Businesses

In the horse business, as in any other type of enterprise, there are three basic business types. This is also known as the legal structure of the business. The three basic types or forms of business are -- sole proprietorships, partnerships, and both C and S forms of corporations. In some states a newer form of business, the limited liability company, is also available. Limited partnerships are another business form, but their use in equine industry is rare. The entrepreneur starting a business should examine the characteristics of each form available and determine which is best suited to his needs.

Generally, people in the horse business must consider the same factors as other business owners in determining the type of business to form. Factors to consider include:

- the tax aspects of each business form;
- the ease of ownership transfer;
- limitations on liability; and
- the entrepreneur's willingness to adhere to the required conditions of the business form, especially corporations.

Good planning during the start-up phase of a business is essential and professionals should be consulted. In fact, a good business plan should budget for these costs right from the onset. Not only should an experienced attorney be consulted, but a good accountant should be a part of the team.

(As will be discussed in Chapter Three, pages 21-28, on taxation Equine Businesses and Taxes.) Proper and careful tax planning should be done at the earliest possible stages of any horse enterprise. When selecting the legal structure or form of business, the business owner will need to make special note of all requirements of each form. This will help ensure that the available benefits will be derived from the legal structure chosen.

Sole Proprietorships

As the name implies, a "sole proprietorship" is when one person owns an entire business. It is literally a "one-man band." It is probably the most common form of business in the horse industry. The main advantages of the sole proprietorship are simplicity and lack of outside interference. Many people in the horse business describe themselves only as horse trainers, breeders, etc., and not business executives. Generally, they do not want others telling them how to run their business, nor do they want to be accountable to partners or shareholders. The sole proprietorship is well suited for horse-related businesses because it is the most flexible form of business.

One of the major advantages of the sole proprietorship form of business can also be one of its greatest disadvantages—it's simplicity. Too much simplicity, especially in the financial area, can damage a sole proprietorship. Horse businesses are very expensive and require a great deal of capital. Since the primary legal characteristic of the sole proprietorship is that the proprietor is personally liable for all business debts, if the business is unable to meet its financial obligations, its creditors may pursue the personal assets of the proprietor. The sole proprietor is generally limited to financing the business by borrowing money. There are no other investors; there is no one else to share in losses, expenses or taxes. When loans are taken out from banks or other lending institutions they require periodic payments, regardless of whether or not the business is making money.

All profits and losses of the business pass through and are reported directly on the proprietor's personal income tax return. No matter how appealing the simplicity, privacy, and flexibility of the sole proprietorship, close examination and long range planning might show that another business structure is more appropriate.

Partnerships

Another common form of business in the horse industry is the "partnership" which simply involves two or more parties agreeing to be partners in a business venture. Partnerships range in scope from literal "one-horse-deals" to those operating the largest horse farms in the country. There are no formal legal requirements for establishing a general partnership, however preparation of a formal partnership agreement serves as a legal document between partners, and is highly advisable

A partnership is generally financed in two ways: First, contributions of capital may be made by the partners. These contributions become partnership property and are subject to the claims of the creditors of the business. Second, the partnership can borrow money. Again, this requires the partnership to make periodic payments to the lender regardless of the partnership's ability to pay. As with sole proprietorships, the partnership form of business has advantages and disadvantages.

On the advantage side, partnerships can be relatively simple both in structure and administration. Unlike corporations, no governmental approval is required of a partnership prior to starting the venture. The formal agreement should be written according to accepted business standards at the start of the business partnership.

Although, from a tax standpoint, partnerships appear to be quite simple, looks can be deceiving. The basic scheme of taxing partnerships is that each partner is taxed on their share of income and can deduct their share of expenses. For example, in an equal partnership of two partners, each is taxed on half of the partnership income and can take half of the partnership's deductions or losses. The partnership itself pays no taxes but is required to file informational tax returns annually with the Internal Revenue Service. In the chapter on taxation some of the problems concerning determination of "profit" and "business versus hobby" will show that even a seemingly simple taxing scheme can be full of difficulties and pitfalls.

Another advantage of a partnership is the ability to raise capital. By bringing others into the partnership, additional financial resources are available to the venture. Also, in a partnership there is an ability to spread the risk of loss. Unlike the "Lone Ranger" aspect of the sole proprietorship, partners bear losses and expenses together, which can be considered to be a prudent business practice.

A major disadvantage of the partnership form of business is that it can be like a marriage—easy to get into and expensive to get out of. Unless the partnership is properly documented with a written agreement, which provides for dissolution of the partnership, it can become a bonanza for lawyers, accountants, appraisers and others. With professional help and planning, many problems can be avoided. This is also the time to ask lots of questions and make sure that any professional involved is familiar with your business circumstances.

Often times a partnership is formed between family members. This formation is convenient, however business agreements between family members holds its own set of problems. Each member may have their own reasons for getting into the business and these differences can cause unresolvable problems. Each member of the partnership should agree on a common goal. This goal may be raising the best horses possible, making a profit, training youth or whatever, as long as the members agree on a common goal and how to reach that goal.

Also, conventional business practices, (a formal accounting system and organized records) along with open lines of communication seem to ease some of these obstacles.

Probably the biggest disadvantage of the partnership form of business is the ability of each partner to bind the partnership to specific obligations. In the eyes of the law, each partner is an agent of the partnership with full power and authority to speak for, and bind the partnership. Unfortunately, it is not uncommon for partners to make commitments on behalf of the partnership which are not in the best interest of the entity or its other partners. This can lead to very serious problems both within the partnership and with outsiders with whom commitments have been made.

In a partnership, there is no limit to a partner's liability as in a corporation. Instead, there is a potential for a broadened exposure to liability. The effects of becoming a partner in the wrong partnership, or with the wrong partners, can spell financial disaster. Not only can one lose his investment in the partnership, he can expose all of his other assets to loss if the partnership becomes obligated to outsiders for losses. To avoid this exposure of personal net worth to possible loss many business people in the horse industry prefer the corporate form of business.

Corporations

Corporations are creatures of the law and require governmental approval before starting the venture. A corporation is formed by filing proposed Articles of Incorporation, usually with the office of the Secretary of State, in the state chosen the be the state of incorporation. A Certificate of Incorporation is subsequently issued by the Secretary of State, and the corporation is then in official existence and can start doing business.

The legal description states that a corporation is owned by its shareholders and is run by a board of directors elected by the shareholders. Anyone receiving compensation from the corporation, including working officers, are considered employees for the purposes of state and federal income tax withholding, unemployment insurance and worker's compensation. (Chapter Two entitled Employer Requirements, pages 13-20, will explain the complex requirements of hiring employees.)

Both legal and accounting participation are required in forming, organizing and utilizing corporations. They are usually more expensive to create and maintain than partnerships.

Depending on the state of incorporation, reports must be prepared and filed every one or two years to the state and a fee paid to maintain the corporation in good standing. Look in the phone book for the local Chamber of Commerce, Small Business Administration or the Office of Regulatory Reform. All can help with licenses and permits for new and expanding businesses. These organizations should also help with federal and state tax requirements for your type of business, unemployment insurance, worker's compensation and registering your business name.

A major advantage of the corporate form of business is the limited liability of shareholders. Unlike partners, shareholders only have the amount of their investment in the corporation at risk. The most they can lose is what they put into the venture.

Another advantage of corporations over the other business forms is that they have perpetual existence in most cases, giving it the power to survive the death of any owner. If a sole proprietor dies, so does his proprietorship, often requiring sale or liquidation of his assets. In the case of a partnership, the death of one of the partners dissolves the partnership, often requiring liquidation and distribution of the deceased partner's share to his estate (however, a well drafted partnership agreement can address this event to ease the burden on the survivors). From the standpoint of its legal existence, a corporation survives the death of one or more of its shareholders and continues.

As in the case of its perpetual existence, a major advantage of the corporate form is the ease of ownership transfer through the sale of stock. Rather than selling the business or reforming a partnership structure, all or any portion of the ownership of a corporation can easily be sold or transferred through the sale or transfer of stock in the corporation. Also, additional capital can more easily be raised by selling stock in the corporation. A corporation can accommodate a larger number of shareholders, further providing a broader base of capital and greatly spreading all risks.

The structured legal requirements governing the activities and administration of the corporation often assist in making business decisions. This is viewed by many as a major advantage of the corporation. Also, the rules and guidelines are more clearly established. The centralized management of the corporation through its board of directors and officers has legally mandated rights and duties. Where partners might encounter difficulty in defining their responsibilities, officers and directors of corporations have more clearly defined roles in the management of the business.

The corporate form is not without its disadvantages. One of the most common problems encountered in a corporation is the legal formality. The law requires meetings, minutes, stock certificates, bylaws, and other corporate records. A corporation requires annual updating of its activities and the maintenance of current, up-to-date records. Also, the fact that corporations are more closely supervised by regulatory bodies such as state agencies and, in some cases the Securities and Exchange Commission, is seen as a disadvantage.

A corporation may acquire the capital necessary to begin and continue operation of the business by two different means. Equity financing involves the issuance of shares of stock, which represent an ownership interest in the business, in exchange for cash, property, labor or services rendered. The primary advantage to the corporation of equity financing is that the corporation is not required to repay the principal or interest. Instead, the shareholder acquires an interest in the business and shares in its future profits. In addition, since the investment received by the corporation constitutes equity, it may be used by the corporation for purposes of acquiring additional capital.

On the other hand, the investor who becomes a shareholder in exchange for his investment has no guarantee of repayment. If the corporation is successful in the future, the shareholder may receive periodic distributions of the corporation's profits in the form of dividends. Dividends are taxable to the shareholder as ordinary income. If the corporation repurchases its shares from the shareholder, the profit from that event is also taxable to the shareholder.

Remember, corporations are more expensive to administer due to the increased formal requirements of maintaining the corporate structure.

There are two types of corporations that are different only in how they are taxed under the Internal Revenue Code. With the exception of how they are taxed, both forms of corporations are treated the same by corporation laws. These types are the C Corporation and the S or Subchapter S Corporation.

C Corporations

The C Corporation gets its name from the fact that it is taxed under Subchapter C of the Internal Revenue Code.

C Corporations are subject to double taxation where profits are taxed at the corporate level and dividends are taxed at the shareholder level. Since this type of corporation is subject to double taxation, when possible, it is avoided in the horse industry. However, when a corporation cannot qualify as a Subchapter S Corporation, the C designation is the only option available. The major advantage of the S Corporation is that this double taxation disadvantage is eliminated.

S Corporations

Under the S Corporation structure, the officers have elected to be taxed like a partnership under the Internal Revenue Code. The corporation itself is not taxed, but each shareholder is taxed on their prorate share of income minus expenses. The Internal Revenue Code sets strict standards for qualifying and electing to be taxed as a Subchapter S Corporation. For instance, all shareholders must agree to elect S Corporation status. This form of business is limited to 35 shareholders who must be U.S. citizens, or can be students from out of the country (aliens). The stock of the corporation cannot be owned by another corporation. There are other requirements regarding the class of stock and earnings which should be fully explained to all potential stockholders. Subchapter S Corporations are quite common in the horse industry. Certainly, like the previous forms of business, corporations have their advantages and disadvantages.

And, now a new option may be available in the form of a Limited Liability Company.

Limited Liability Company

Recently eight states (Kansas, Colorado, Florida, Utah, Virginia, Nevada, Wyoming, and Texas) have enacted legislation creating a new type of business, the Limited Liability Company (LLC). This legislation gives the owner of a business, including horse businesses, an entirely new option in the formation of a business. The LLC is neither a corporation nor a partnership, but can offer some of the advantages of both types of business structures without being burdened by some of their disadvantages. The Limited Liability Company is a unique business entity that, like Subchapter S Corporations combines the tax benefits of a partnership with the limited liability benefits of a corporation.

An LLC is formed by one or more organizers files Articles of Organization with the Secretary of State. These articles are very similar to corporate Articles of Incorporation and include: the name of the LLC; the period of its duration; name and address of its registered agent; the names and addresses of the initial manager or managers; and, if desired, any delayed effective date of its creation. The name must contain the words "limited liability company" or the abbreviation thereof, LLC.

The owners of an LLC are called "members." They have certain voting rights including: the right to unanimously approve transfers of interests by other members; the right to vote for managers of the LLC; and, if the articles so provide, the right to unanimously consent to continuation of the LLC on the death, retirement, expulsion, resignation, bankruptcy, or dissolution of a member. The members have the right to any other matter provided in the operating agreement, and all votes require a majority or unanimous vote, consent, or agreement of the members. New members may be admitted only upon the unanimous written consent of all existing members. The LLC is managed by one or more managers who are elected annually by a vote of the members. The operating agreement is much like a partnership agreement and it may contain provisions concerning such matters as the purposes of the LLC, the election and duties of the managers, sharing of profits and losses, distributions, etc.. A properly drafted operating agreement should state how the company is to be managed, and how profits and losses will be allocated among the members of the LLC.

Probably the most significant characteristic of a LLC is that of limited liability. The legislation contains a specific provision that the members and managers are not liable "under a judgement, decree, or order of a court, or in any other manner, for a debt, obligation, or liability of the limited liability company." However, as with corporations, a member is personally liable to the LLC to perform any promise to contribute cash or property. Also, members must return any distribution they received from the LLC when its liabilities exceed its assets, and this liability extends for a period of six years after such improper distribution is made. Another six year period of a member's liability is imposed for the amount of a member's contribution that has been returned, only to the extent necessary to discharge liabilities which existed during the period the contribution was held by the LLC. Legislation provides that the doctrine of "piercing the corporate veil" will be applicable to LLCs as it presently is applied to corporations. This gives creditors the right, in certain cases where the entity is a sham, to proceed directly against members for the debts, obligations, and liabilities of the entity.

Limited Liability Companies enjoy the same tax treatment as partnerships. Like a partnership, the LLC is not a separate taxable entity between its members and the government, and income as well as losses flow directly from the LLC to its members/owners without subjecting them to double taxation as in the case of non-partnership for purposes of state income taxation.

While including many of the benefits of a Subchapter S Corporation, the LLC does not include the stringent requirements for membership as a Subchapter S Corporation imposes on its stockholders. For example, a LLC is allowed an unlimited number of members where a Subchapter S Corporation is limited to 35 shareholders. Also, membership in an LLC is not limited to United States citizens, while a Subchapter S Corporation may not have foreign shareholders.

The LLC is a new and appealing alternative to conventional forms of equine businesses. It grants both limited liability and favorable tax treatment while avoiding many of the restrictive requirements imposed on Subchapter S Corporations. However, LLCs are presently authorized in only eight states, and in an age of interstate and international business, this presents problems of legal recognition. While LLCs may not be appropriate for every equine business situation, the fact of their existence and availability in, at present, eight states should make them a consideration for many horsemen.

Syndications

Syndications are similar to a partnership between two or more persons regarding the ownership of a stallion, broodmares, race or show horses. Syndications should be written agreements, whereby each partner will benefit from their share in the ownership of the animal. This benefit may be breeding rights or a share of the winnings, but the details should always be clearly spelled out in a written contract. A syndication can legally take one of two forms. It may be in the form of a partnership or a co-ownership.

A syndication can be a co-ownership, however this is less likely because a co-owner may not sell breeding rights. Caution is advised in syndications because of something called an "investment security." Selling unregistered securities is a criminal act under federal law. It is punishable by a fine of up to $10,000, imprisonment for five years, or both. A syndication is an excellent example of a situation needing legal counsel.

This chapter has briefly introduced the four main forms of business in the horse industry. As mentioned, always obtain competent legal and other professional help when selecting the best structure for your equine business. Every case is different and requires individual analysis and treatment. Remember, the best law is preventative law. Obtain the necessary legal, accounting or other professional advice before finally selecting the business form or making any commitments. Plan carefully and plan ahead.

Chapter 2

Employer Requirements

As with any growing business, you may at some point find yourself hiring employees. Employees are a major concern and the specifics of the horse industry will only complicate things.

The question becomes, "Do you hire full- or part- time employees, or do you hire subcontractors to perform specific jobs on an as-needed basis?" If you hire contract labor, your paperwork life is much easier. But just calling someone contract labor doesn't make them so. And if you incorrectly classify those working for you, you may end up paying some big dollars to the IRS and to the state.

It is important to first recognize the traits of a typical employee/employer relationship. The following guidelines will help you determine whether or not you have a typical employee/employer relationship as defined by the laws of most states. (All of them do not have to apply):

- Job training is necessary
- Supervision and payroll responsibilities are the employer's responsibility
- Employer sets the work hours
- All work time must be devoted to the employer
- Work-place is restricted (i.e. must work on site)
- Prioritization of the work is done by employer

- Payment is made by the hour or some type of salary arrangement
- Employer pays expenses incurred on the job
- The employee will not incur any financial losses
- The same job cannot be performed for another employer
- The worker can quit without recourse from the employer

The above traits may commonly apply to a stable-cleaner, groom or handyman as a typical employer/employee relationship. A trainer or horseshoer will usually be classified as a contractor because they perform their jobs using more of the guidelines mentioned below. The guidelines for a contractor are as follows:

- Work is done by the project
- The contractor determines the tasks to be accomplished and the order in which they are to be accomplished
- Establishes his or her own working hours
- Works for others at the same time
- Uses own equipment, tools

If you have any questions - call someone from an appropriate government agencies found in the phone book, the local chamber of commerce or the Small Business Administration. This is why we pay taxes for government agencies like, the Department of Labor and Employment.

For both employees and contract labor there will be federal and state forms to contend with. For a contract laborer, you must keep track of the exact amount paid. Then at the end of the year, fill out a 1099 form for each individual paid over $600 during the year.

Employees will require the following forms:

Federal Forms

Form SS-4

The federal form SS-4 is the application for a federal employer identification number (F.E.I.N.) used to set up income tax withholding, FICA and FUTA, through the IRS. For immediate help obtaining a F.E.I.N. call (801) 625-7645 during regular business hours. This is a toll call and you will read your completed SS-4 form over the phone. (Perhaps this office will get a fax machine in the near future.) A F.E.I.N. will be assigned to you and your completed SS-4 form must be mailed within five days.

Form W-4

Each employee must sign a completed and dated W-4. This form should be included in the employee's personnel file. The W-4 tells the employer how many exemptions to consider when withholding federal income tax from payroll checks. Having this form on file is not only required by the government, but is also the employer's insurance policy against disputes that could arise later with the IRS or the employee. The W-4 is required to be filed with the IRS only in special circumstances.

INS Form I-9

Another item for the personnel file is the Immigration and Naturalization Service's (INS) form I-9. This form was devised to ensure that employers do not hire illegal aliens. The paperwork is not difficult, but is required. This form must be completed within three working days after employment begins, and if the documents cannot be presented, call the state INS office regarding the 90 day extension.

The requirements explain that the employer make a photocopy of the INS form and the support documents (U.S. Passport and a State Driver's License), and keep them in the employee's file. The employee must present identification and proof of employability within the United States. The items in list A, establish both identity and employment eligibility. The items in list B only prove identity and the items in list C only verify employment eligibility.

INS Support Documents

List A:

1. U.S. Passport (unexpired or expired)

2. Certificate of U.S. Citizenship (INS Form N-560 or N-561)

3. Certificate of Naturalization (INS Form N-550 or N-570)

4. Unexpired foreign passport, with I-551 stamp or attached INS Form I-94 indicating unexpired employment authorization

5. Alien Registration Receipt Card with photograph (INS Form I-151 or I-551)

6. Unexpired Temporary Resident Card (INS Form I-688)

7. Unexpired Employment Authorization Card (INS Form I-688-A)

8. Unexpired Reentry Permit (INS Form I-327)

9. Unexpired Refugee Travel Document (INS Form I-571)

10. Unexpired Employment Authorization Document issued by the INS which contains a photograph (INS Form I-688B)

List B:

1. State or Canadian driver's license or ID card with photo

2. Voter's registration

3. School I.D. card with photo

4. U.S. Military card or draft record or Military dependent's ID card

5. Native American tribal document

List C:

1. Social Security card

2. Certified copy of birth certificate

3. Native American tribal document

4. INS Form I-197

The penalties for failing to comply with this requirement begin at $250 for each unauthorized employee and can quickly reach $10,000 per violation. The possibility of incurring thousands of dollars in fines certainly justifies the extra trouble of compliance.

For further information, contact the local INS office.

Quarterly Payroll Reports

Two quarterly payroll reports must be filed each calendar quarter. When filing employee forms information regarding the payment schedule (usually forms and envelopes) for quarterly Payroll Reports will be mailed to the business address. The employer is required to understand the forms and file the reports on or before the stated due date.

There are many accounting or bookkeeping services offering to prepare payroll and file the necessary forms. The exact extent of each bookkeeping service and fees charged can be obtained by calling businesses specializing in bookkeeping services. (More information regarding bookkeeping services and requirements will be covered in chapter four, Bookkeeping Procedures.)

Form 941

The purpose of this form is to report the amount of wages, federal income tax, and Social Security tax applicable to your business to the IRS. This form tells the IRS what your payroll tax liability was for the quarter and when it was due for payment.

Note: Your payroll deposits should be made payable to your bank using Form 8109. On the back of Form 941 you will find a schedule showing how often the deposits need to be made.

Form 940

This report gives the year's total federal unemployment tax (FUTA) liability for the company's payroll. If you pay wages of $1,500 or more, or have at least one employee for part of a week in 20 different weeks, you are subject to file. All wages are subject to FUTA. If you owe more than $100 FUTA tax at the end of the calendar quarter, you must deposit the tax with an authorized bank by using the federal tax deposit coupon that will be sent to you by the IRS. The annual return, Federal Form 940, must be filed by January 31 of the next year.

Form W-2

Employers are responsible for reporting payroll information to the Social Security Administration and to employees with W-2 forms.

Note: Owners of sole-proprietorships and partnerships cannot be classified as employees. Owners of corporations, however, can. These forms are to be sent to the Social Security Administration, not the IRS at the end of the year.

State Requirements

Each state will have different reporting requirements. Check with your state government offices, along with city and county offices, for specific requirements. Ignorance is not considered an excuse.

Unemployment Insurance

Unemployment Insurance is a fund established by law to pay benefits to employees who lose their jobs though no fault of their own. All unemployment insurance funds are paid by employers in the form of unemployment insurance taxes.

Your company is liable for unemployment as soon as you hire an employee. Some non-profit, agricultural and domestic employers have slightly different standards. Check your state requirements.

If an employee files for unemployment, an employer may contest, stating that the employee is not entitled to unemployment insurance.

If the employee is at fault for their termination, they may be refused unemployment payments, thus saving the company a claim. The burden of proof is on the employer based on documentation of performance and the reason for termination. All of this should be in writing and in the file of the employee prior to letting the employee go.

Worker's Compensation

Worker's Compensation is insurance that employers must obtain to provide coverage for employee medical costs and compensation for time missed from work due to a job related injury or occupational disease. All premium costs are paid by the employers.

Employers are responsible for the coverage of both full-time and part-time employees, as well as in contract laborers in some cases. Before a contract laborer begins working for you it is important to discuss the subject of insurance coverage, especially worker's compensation coverage. For example, if you hire a painter to paint your home and barn and he falls off of the ladder and is injured, you could be responsible for the medical bills and lost income due to his inability to earn a living. That is, unless his company, (i.e. Joe's Paint and Repair) has insurance coverage including worker's compensation. It is in your best interest to ask to see a copy of the insurance binder before you hire an independent contractor.

As this text is being written, many state horse associations and councils are working to bring the insurance rates for worker's compensation down for the horse industry. The American Horse Council, along with associated state councils, work with legislators on government policies effecting the horse industry.

Check your state's requirements for worker's compensation and filing dates. Check with your state horsemen's association for equine-specific information regarding worker's compensation.

There are other responsibilities employers need to be concerned with. If you are large enough to have 20 employees or more, you will have to comply with "COBRA" (the Consolidated Budget Reconciliation Act of 1985). This new requirement concerns employer-provided group health plans. There are also employer posting requirements. The posters range from Anti-Discrimination posters, Safety posters, Equal Opportunity posters and more.

Managing employees is very different from riding and enjoying horses. The decision to hire full- or part-time employees is a large step for some equine businesses and all options should be considered carefully.

Chapter 3

Equine Businesses and Taxes

The forms of horse businesses are very important, but from a tax standpoint, the EXISTENCE of the business is probably the most important aspect of its business standing. Owning and keeping horses is very expensive. It is natural that horse owners would want to deduct as many of the expenses as possible. In years past (prior to the recent tax reform acts) the horse industry was notorious for its tax shelters. The business also was appealing to many wealthy horse lovers who benefited from the deductions. The Internal Revenue Service (IRS) targeted the horse industry for review and established unique standards and regulations to prevent abuses. The question became whether the horse enterprise was a business or was it a hobby?

Section 183 of the Internal Revenue Code provides that an individual or Subchapter S corporation cannot deduct expenses which are greater than the income from an activity, if that activity is "not engaged in for profit." This provision is referred to as the "hobby loss" provision. It means that losses from a horse activity cannot be deducted against income from other sources unless the horse activity is a "business" and not a "hobby."

It is very common for horse owners to begin as hobbyists. They enjoy riding, buy a horse and become addicted. Initially their interest in horses is financed by their other income. As the new owner's activities multiply and expand, expenses also increase. The point is reached when the horse owner asks, "When can I deduct these expenses?" The answer under the tax laws is, "When your horse activities become a business and not a hobby."

Under the law, hobby losses are deductible only to the extent of income from the hobby activity, and are thus, very limited. The ultimate question in business versus hobby cases is whether the taxpayer entered into and continued the activity with the OBJECTIVE OF MAKING A PROFIT. Of course, it is easy to say that any horse activity had a profit making objective. The Internal Revenue Service has established tests, other than the mere statement of the horse owner, to establish whether an activity had a valid objective of making a profit.

The Two of Seven Presumption

The two of seven presumption was formulated by the Internal Revenue Service for exclusive application to horse activities. The Tax Code provides that if an activity shows two profit years within a seven year period (starting with the first profit year), the activity will be presumed to be a business venture. This "two of seven" rule only creates a presumption that the horse activity is a business, and the I.R.S. can attempt to rebut the presumption by taking the position that the activity was really a hobby. If this occurs, the burden is on the I.R.S. to show that the facts and circumstances still indicate that there was "no profit motive" in spite of the fact that the horse person made a profit two years out of seven in the activity. Other tests and factors are used by the IRS and the Courts to determine whether a profit motive is truly present in the horse activity so that the applicability of the "two of seven" can be determined. There are nine (9) factors in the Internal Revenue Service regulations used to determine if a horse activity is engaged in for profit. The factors are as follows:

1. The manner in which the activity is conducted. Keeping good books and records and using businesslike methods is essential.

2. The horse person's expertise, or that of his advisor, is examined. Research and study into the economics of the horse activity by the horse person or the advisors, and the utilization of this information in the conduct of the activity are evidence of a profit motive.

3. The time and effort expended in the activity is important. Devoting considerable personal time to the horse activity, especially if the activity does not have substantial personal or recreational aspects, can indicate the horse person's intent to make a profit. Partial or total withdrawal from another occupation to devote time to the horse operation, may be evidence that it is engaged in for profit.

4. The expectation that the assets used in the horse activity may appreciate in value. The I.R.S. regulations provide that the term "profit" includes appreciation in the value of assets, including land, used in the activity. Thus, even if no profit is derived from the current operations, an overall profit may result if the appreciation in the value of the horses, the land, or other assets used in the horse activity is taken into account, along with the current income from the activity.

5. The taxpayer's success in similar operations is a factor for consideration. If the taxpayer has made similar unprofitable horse activities profitable in the past, a profit motive could be present in the current operation.

6. The taxpayer's history of income or losses from the activity, including the two of seven year test, is another important factor. Internal Revenue Service regulations provide that a SERIES OF PROFIT YEARS is strong evidence that the horse activity is engaged in for profit. It is acknowledged that a series of loss-years during the starting stages of a horse operation is not unusual. However, if losses continue beyond the period normally required to make similar operations profitable, this can lead to a conclusion that the activity is not engaged in for profit. Unforeseen circumstances, such as disease, natural disaster, or a depressed market, can be taken into account under this factor.

7. The amount of occasional profit, if any, earned by the horse operation is also examined. The ratio of profits to losses is an important element in this factor. It is quite easy to lose money and quite difficult to make money in the horse business. The Internal Revenue regulations provide that an occasional small profit from an activity which generates large losses will not be determinative that the activity is a business. However, the regulation also provides that "an opportunity to earn a substantial ultimate profit in a highly speculative venture is ordinarily sufficient to indicate that the activity is engaged in for profit, even though losses or occasional small profits are actually generated." This statement seems to apply directly to the horse business.

8. The financial status of the taxpayer is another factor. If a taxpayer does not have substantial income from other sources, this could indicate that his horse operation is engaged in for profit.

9. The elements of personal pleasure or recreation are the final factor. I.R.S. regulations provide that personal motives in carrying on an activity may indicate the activity is not engaged in for profit, especially where there are recreational or personal elements involved. However, an activity will not be treated as a hobby merely because the taxpayer has purposes in addition to making a profit. In other words, it is fine to enjoy the horses, provided other factors indicate the presence of a profit motive.

According to the Internal Revenue Service, any one of these factors is not more important than another. All factors are considered in determining whether the activity qualifies as a "business" for tax purposes or whether it is a "hobby."

Cases interpreting and deciding whether particular operations are businesses or hobby activities are often ultimately decided by the United State Tax Court. The following cases show how the nine factors weigh in the analysis of horse operations involving business versus hobby issues.

Mills v. Commissioner (T.C. Memo 1990-432) This case involved a physician who initially bought an Arabian horse for his daughter, became interested in breeding Arabians and ultimately owned 69 horses over a ten year period. The Tax Court held against the taxpayer's contention that the breeding operation was a business. The Court reviewed the nine factors and found that they were not present in the doctor's favor. It found that he did not carry on the activity in a businesslike manner, made poor breeding decisions, did not keep good records, made no attempt to cut expenses and maximize income his large income from his medical practice allowed him to operate at a loss, and his personal contact with the operation was in connection with its more pleasurable aspects.

Stephens v. Commissioner (T.C. 1990-376) was a case won by the taxpayer. In that case, the Tax Court found that the taxpayer's operation was a business. Stephens was a full-time employee of the Ford Motor Company who decided to raise Quarter horses. He had previously studied vocational agriculture and had worked with horses on his family's farm when he was young. When Stephens started his breeding operation, he consulted professionals who helped him formulate a business plan. He concentrated his efforts in establishing a small, quality broodmare operation. The taxpayer kept excellent records of every event of significance to his business. Mr. Stephens devoted substantial time and effort to the operation, both before and after work and on the weekends. The Court was impressed that not all of Mr. Stephen's participation was pleasurable when it stated in its opinion that, "on those occasions when he had to sleep in the barn in order to be near a foaling mare, he must have concluded that the enjoyment was completely eliminated."

Seebold v. Commissioner (T.C. Memo 1988-183) involved a case where the Tax Court found that the taxpayer's operation was a business operated with the intention of making a profit even though it has shown no profit. The Seebolds became interested in Appaloosa horses, first for pleasure, then later as a business. The taxpayers consulted with several knowledgeable horse people in starting their activity. The Tax Court reviewed the nine factors in the regulations and found in favor of the taxpayers. The Court found that the operation was conducted in a businesslike manner; the Seebolds had worked hard to develop their expertise in the horse business more than 40 hours a week were devoted to the horse activity; there was the potential for one of the taxpayer's horses to appreciate in value through extensive training, thus ultimately increasing the amount of stud fee that could be charged and the value of his offspring; the Seebold's losses were predictable start-up losses and, although no profit had been made, they were projecting a modest profit in 1987. The taxpayer's income from other sources was modest when compared with the losses generated by the horse operation, a fact when coupled with the Seebold's intention to make their Appaloosa activity a source of income in later years, suggested that a profit motive existed; and, finally, the Court was influenced by the fact that the taxpayers did not operate the activity for pleasure or recreation, and the way they conducted the operation, a great deal of effort, devotion, and hard work was necessary.

From these cases it is very apparent that there is no easy test for determining whether a horse operation will qualify as a business. Each case is judged on its individual facts and circumstances, applying the nine factors found in the regulations. Again, expert professional assistance is necessary and can pay great dividends.

Passive Activity Losses

Probably the implementation of the limits on passive activity losses in the Tax Reform Act of 1986 has had the most direct impact on the horse industry. For a number of years the horse business benefitted from the investment capital in it by people who, because of their high tax brackets, needed to shelter large sums of income. The substantial deductions from horse operations afforded these individuals the opportunity to avoid significant tax liability. The horse business benefitted from the infusion of capital and, in many cases, by the lack of concern over the amount of losses and deductions generated by the business. Obviously, in these cases, profit was not a motive.

In Section 469 of the Act, Congress virtually eliminated these tax shelter benefits. This section provided that deductions from passive business activities may not be deducted from other income. The large investment in horse operations as tax shelters became unattractive to high-bracket taxpayers, and the horse industry lost a major source of capital investment.

The Internal Revenue Code now provides that a taxpayer must "materially participate" in the activity for the activity to be "nonpassive" and to exclude it from the passive activity limitations. "Material participation" is defined as regular, continuous and substantial involvement in the operations of an activity. This concept is relatively new and has not yet been fully clarified and defined by court decision or regulation.

The Internal Revenue Service has adopted some regulations that serve as guidelines to aid in determining when a horse person's participation in an activity will be deemed to be "material." Among these standards are tests of the number of hours the taxpayer devotes to the activity. For example, at least 100 hours of participation in the activity is required during the tax year. Very recently, the IRS has proposed regulations which attempt to explain whether various equine activities will be treated as one activity for purposes of computing the 100 hour test. These proposed regulations address the problems of taxpayers whose equine activities include a breeding business and a separate training or boarding enterprise and who seek to combine their hours spent at each to satisfy the test. The regulations provide that whether activities can be combined or must be treated as separate activities depends upon the relevant facts and circumstances, to include: (1) similarities of the types of the activities, (2) control, (3) common ownership, (4) geographical location of the activities, and (5) the interdependencies of the activities. The new regulations and their applicability require current expert analysis and advice. Other standards require the taxpayer to be active at least five years or material participation by the owner out of the last ten years.

The Internal Revenue Code requires a significant commitment of time by the taxpayer in some substantial activity in order to avoid the passive activity limitation. This area, like most other areas of the horse business, requires expert consultation. The regulations and interpretations are complex and technical. The counsel of professionals is necessary if a taxpayer is going to pursue avoidance of Section 469. While it may not be necessary for the taxpayer to have "dirt under his fingernails and manure on his boots," it certainly wouldn't hurt.

Chapter 4

Bookkeeping Procedures

Since business people and "hobby" horse owners are under the watchful eye of the Internal Revenue Service, it is imperative that individuals who wish to be successful in the horse industry keep good records. It is important to develop an accurate, functional, easy system of record keeping prior to starting up the horse business.

All equine businesses should have the following items in their bookkeeping system:

- Detailed operating statements
- Comparison of current results to budgets and prior periods
- Financial statements
- Information for tax returns and reports to regulatory agencies
- Sufficient control to protect assets and detect errors

The prospective equine business owner needs to review the following items:

- What form of business was chosen; Sole Proprietorship, Partnership, Corporation or LLC.
- Industry standards
- Number of employees, now and in the future
- The requirements of the location and if the location would ever move or have a second location

Experts recommend that the first step in setting up a bookkeeping system is the selection of the tax year or year-end. The term tax year refers to the annual accounting period. The selection of a year end is sometimes dictated by form of ownership. For instance, a regular Corporation has no specific restriction, while an S Corporation and Partnership usually must follow a calendar year. Be sure to consult with an expert before making a decision, as tax laws tend to change.

The second step is to select a method of accounting. The two most common are the cash method and the accrual method. The cash method recognizes income and expenses based on when cash is received or disbursed. It provides the most flexible means of deferring taxable income into future tax years. The accrual method recognizes income and expenses based on when income is earned or an obligation to pay a debt is incurred. It generally provides better matching of revenue and expenditures.

The green ledgers or accounting journals found at office supply stores can provide an inexpensive organized format to begin keeping records. Some of these ledgers even have suggested column headings to remind you to keep track of the date the money came in, who it is from, the amount received and if there is any sales tax to be collected. The cash paid out side of the ledger has even more columns which not only track the amount paid out, but to whom, and even suggestions for tracking where the money is being spent, i.e. salaries and wages, telephone and rent, office supplies, advertising, taxes and more.

During the start-up stage of your business you will want to contact an accountant, the Small Business Administration (or the Service Corps of Retired Executives, SCORE), your local community college or continuing education program for consulting. Make sure that your accounting methods fit your needs. You may want to add special entries in your ledger for the equine-related publications you subscribe to, memberships including; the American Quarter Horse

Association (AQHA), International Arabian Horse Association (IAHA), American Horse Show Association (AHSA), American Horse Council (AHC), etc. and special promotional expenses such as showing horses.

Once a method of accounting is adopted, it can be changed only with IRS permission. Permission is usually granted in the case of switching from the cash method to the accrual, and routinely denied in the reverse.

The most common mistake made when setting up a bookkeeping system in the horse industry happens when the business owner doesn't understand the importance of a bookkeeping system and ignores the need. Such business owners tend to use the shoebox method as they allow receipts and invoices to build up in piles or boxes. The second mistake is overkill. Although not nearly as frequent, overkill occurs when owners invest a fortune in complicated hardware and software, but then realize it is too complicated to utilize effectively or it doesn't meet the needs of the business owner.

Today's business world offers more options with respect to who will keep the books. The three most prominent options are:

Keep them yourself: This should be the choice if the business is extremely simple, has few employees, a single location and if it requires a small amount of time. If this method is chosen, accountants recommend using a calendar year and a cash accounting method. This simplifies the use of the "Schedule C" form used in tax preparation.

Bookkeeping services: These services usually compile receipts, canceled checks, check stubs, then process the data and prepare financial statements. If the system is simple and outside reports are infrequent, a bookkeeper may be all that is needed. When choosing any type of bookkeeping service, make sure they understand the horse business, tax regulations which apply to the business and that you are knowledgeable enough to check their work.

Bookkeeper/Accountant: More complex systems generally require an accountant. In today's economy, it is possible to find someone willing to work evenings or part-time to help with the costs of starting a business. Again, make sure they understand the horse business, tax regulations which apply to the business and that you are willing to become knowledgeable enough to check their work.

Chapter 5

Collection of Debts

People involved in the horse business, just like those involved in other businesses, often have trouble collecting debts owed to them. Whether it is bills for boarding or training horses, shoeing, veterinary services, feed bills, or other facets of the horse business, getting paid can be a problem. Collection of debts is more laborious in difficult economic times. Unlike other businesses the horse industry often does not allow many discretionary purchases. Horses must be fed, cared for and treated by veterinarians. These necessary services, even in hard times, require that the provider be paid.

There are a number of methods available in attempting to collect debts. These range from hiring an attorney or collection agency to self-help attempts by the creditor. As expected, the more expensive way of debt collection is by utilizing the services of a professional. Attorneys will charge either an hourly fee or a percentage of the amount collected, plus costs in either case. Hourly rates for lawyers can range from a lower range of $60 to $100 per hour to higher amounts of $125 to $175 per hour. Regarding the selection of an attorney, a client should always know and agree to the lawyer's fees prior to actually retaining the attorney. Percentage fees by attorneys also can range from lows of ten percent (10%) to twenty-five percent (25%), to a high of forty percent (40%). The client must know and agree to, preferably in writing, any percentage fee to avoid later difficulties.

Collection agencies generally use a fee structure based on a percentage of what is collected. It is quite common to see a graduated scale of fee arrangement used by these agencies.

In the case of both agencies and lawyers, the client/creditor is responsible for the payment of all costs. These will vary depending on whether or not a suit is filed or if there is difficulty in serving the debtor with legal process.

In cases where the person decides to use professional collectors, a number of things must still be done by the client.

1. First, the creditor must provide the necessary evidence to prove the case. This can be done by furnishing bills, contracts, purchase orders and other documents common in business transactions to show that there was a sale or that services were performed and the debtor was notified of the amount that was due for the goods or service. Copies of any correspondence, or telephone memorandums, should also be organized and furnished to the professional collector for later use in preparing the case.

2. Second, the client should make himself available to meet with the agency or the lawyer to assist in preparing and organizing the case against the debtor. This can also mean appearing in court and testifying at the trial, if necessary.

3. Third, the creditor should keep an open mind in listening to the professional's suggestions on settlement or resolution of the claim. Although most business people want to have every penny due them, this is not always possible. The old adage, "A bird in the hand is worth two in the bush," has wisdom and merit in many cases. Professional collectors can often evaluate chances of recovery and negotiate settlements better than amateurs. In many cases, a professional is best able to gain maximum dollars from the debtors. These are some of the main reasons for considering professional assistance in collecting larger debts.

In contacting any debtor, all creditors must be aware of the existence and effect of both FAIR DEBT COLLECTION ACTS that have been enacted by Congress and the various states. These acts are designed to ensure fair debt collection practices. Although they principally apply to collection agencies, they also apply to creditors who attempt to collect the debt in any other name than their own. Some of the state acts expand the definition of a "debt collector" to include any creditor who is attempting to collect a debt. The laws set forth very strict definitions for creditors and debt collectors and provide both civil and criminal penalties for violation.

The basic purposes of these laws is to eliminate abusive debt collection practices, and protect consumers against debt collection abuses. The laws require that notice of the debt be given the debtor, and sets forth restrictions against threatening or abusive behavior by creditors in attempting to collect. Also, communications with third parties by creditors is subject to strict regulations. Any creditor who attempts to collect his or her own debts must be aware of the existence of the laws stemming from the Fair Debt Collection Acts and avoid any prohibited conduct.

Of course, the business person has other options available to him to collect debts. The most common collection attempt is to contact the debtor and remind them of the bill and try to discover why they have not paid. If the reason for non-payment is dissatisfaction with the service or the merchandise, perhaps some adjustment or minor accommodation will lead to payment. If financial difficulty is the reason for failure to pay the debt, a method of payment over a period of time or receiving a promissory note (Which provides for the payment, interest and attorneys fees if collection suit is necessary) can lead to satisfaction of the debt. Obviously, these methods are successful only if the parties are dealing in good faith and are not trying to ignore or avoid paying the obligation.

Even when it becomes apparent that the debtor is simply trying to avoid paying, the creditor still has some options available to try to collect the debt short of hiring professionals. The most common is the Small Claims Court. This court has limited jurisdiction and can handle cases up to a certain dollar amount. This amount depends on the law of the various states, but it is common to have Small Claims Courts with jurisdictions ranging from $1,000 to $5,000. Local laws should be consulted when considering the filing of a case.

Small Claims Courts have many advantages to the general public including the modest cost in filing a suit, and the prompt hearing of cases. A big advantage to these courts is that usually attorneys are not allowed to represent parties in the court. People represent themselves and present their own cases and defenses. This option can represent a considerable savings for a simple case with adequate documentation. The Small Claims Courts aims to present a fair and impartial forum for the resolution of disputes between people, without unnecessary delay and expense. The court proceeding or trial is less formal than the usual trial, with each side presenting his or her case. At the close of the presentation the court makes its ruling. Unlike more formal trials, when the parties leave the courtroom they know who won and who lost. The rulings are usually clear and understandable, and the parties have "had their day in court."

However, in all collection proceedings, whether professionally done or through the use of a small claims procedure, additional steps are often necessary for the winning party to collect the judgment. People are often surprised that the Court does not go out and collect what it ordered the creditor to pay. The court's job is to hear the evidence presented by both sides and, based on that evidence, make a decision. If a party sues a debtor and the court rules that the debt is due and owing, it will grant the creditor a judgment in the amount of the debt, plus court costs. (attorney fees, in certain limited cases, especially where there was a contract between the parties or a promissory note that was the basis for the suit and which allowed for the court to assess the losing party with the winner's attorney fees are also awarded). Once this judgment is entered by the court, it is up to the winning party to collect. The judgment only gives the prevailing party the right to collect the amount of the judgment.

Common Collection Procedures

This chapter is not intended to be an exhaustive course on how to collect a debt. The laws of the states vary, and local laws must always be consulted. Also, it is recommended that professional advice be obtained before deciding on or attempting any legal proceedings or procedures. However, the following is a brief description of some of the common procedures available in collecting after obtaining a judgment:

1. **LEVYING ON PROPERTY** -- in most states, the real and personal property is subject to execution to apply to a judgment. However, the law provides certain exemptions on parts of the debtor's property, limiting the effect of this procedure to some extent. For example, there are exemptions and limitations on levying on a debtor's residence, on real estate that is subject to a homestead exemption (which in theory preserves a home for the debtor), and on personal property necessary for the debtor to support himself and his family. Also, a debtor's clothing, tools of his trade or profession, family mementoes, and vehicles used for gainful employment are usually exempt from execution. Most state laws also exempt household goods up to a specific value from levy. State and federal law should always be consulted to determine limitations on levying on the property of a judgment debtor. Of course, property that is pledged or mortgaged prior to obtaining the judgment is taken subject to the mortgage. In other words, the security interest of the bank or other lender in a debtor's property is pro-

tected from execution in most cases. All non-exempt property that has not been previously pledged is subject to execution, including corporate stock, bank accounts, cash and bonds.

The process for turning property which has been levied upon into cash to apply to satisfaction of the judgment is governed by law. Usually the sale is conducted by a sheriff or other official (or court appointed officer) and, after deducting the expenses of the sale, the proceeds are turned over to the judgment creditor to apply to the judgment. Again, state and federal laws must be consulted in determining both the method of execution and sale of seized property.

2. **ATTACHMENT** -- is a legal process which allows a defendant's non-exempt property to be taken into custody to obtain jurisdiction over the property or to give security to satisfy a plaintiff's claim if he recovers a judgment.

   Attachment procedures are created by statute which must be strictly followed. It is a procedure that is used by attorneys and other professionals mainly to obtain jurisdiction over an out-of-state party or to create security for a future judgment. Attachment is most commonly done prior to filing suit.

3. **GARNISHMENT** -- is a proceeding where a judgment creditor obtains property or money of the judgment debtor which is held by a third party. Most commonly, the "property or money" are wages or payments due, and the "third party" is the debtor's employer or one who owes him money for goods or services. Garnishment is a method of collecting to satisfy a judgment and requires strict compliance with the appropriate statutes.

As in the case of Attachment or Levy on Property, certain exemptions apply under both state and federal law to garnishment. These exemptions principally apply to wages and earnings of a debtor. The law seeks to avoid making a debtor completely destitute. Therefore, a certain percentage of his earnings are exempt from execution or garnishment. However, as to non-exempt earnings, garnishment can be a very effective method of collecting a judgment.

Briefly, a garnishment is accomplished by serving a legal document (sometimes called a "Writ of Garnishment") on the employer or other party who holds the money or property of the debtor. The employer or other party must respond to the court and the creditor within a certain period of time, stating how much of the debtor's money or property they are holding. After this response, the third party then must pay either into the court or to the debtor, depending on the state law, the non-exempt property of the debtor to be applied to the amount of the judgment. The law of some states provides that these Writs of Garnishment are continuing. This means that until the judgment is satisfied, the employer or third person must pay the non-exempt amount each payday or each time they possess any money or property of the debtor. Again, the laws of the states vary on the subject of garnishment, and a lawyer should be consulted. However, this is one of the most effective and common ways of collecting judgments.

In all collection proceedings there is one overriding matter that brings everything to a stop -- bankruptcy. If a debtor files for any form of bankruptcy during any stage of collection proceedings, no further action can be taken. Exclusive jurisdiction over the debtor's financial affairs is taken over by the United States Bankruptcy Court, and its designated Trustee. All attempts to collect take the form of filing claims against the bankrupt estate. Secured claims, such as mortgages or deeds of trust, are given priority and are paid first. All other unsecured claims are paid out of the remaining assets, if any. In cases of bankruptcy, unsecured creditors are lucky to receive anything.

4. THE AGISTER'S LIEN

In the livestock business, including horses, there exists a legal right and procedure that should be discussed. This is known as the AGISTER'S LIEN. It is a statutory lien for the amount due to those who feed, herd, pasture, keep, board, or provide veterinary care to horses and other livestock. Agister's Liens are created by and interpreted under the laws of the various states. Again, the law of the particular state must be consulted to determine the existence and scope of its agister's lien laws. The law of Colorado and most other states has long provided that an agister have a lien against the livestock for the cost of the care provided to it. If this cost is not paid by the animal's owner, the agister can, after following proper statutory procedure, sell the animal and apply the proceedings against the debt. The basic requirements to perfect an agister's lien are:

1. Exclusive possession of the animal(s) on which the lien is claimed.

2. The animal(s) are not stolen.

3. The agistor has no ownership interest in the animal(s), such as being a partner.

Anyone who owns horses or is in the horse business should know about agistor's liens and their effect. The agister's lien can be a powerful tool for stable keepers, veterinarians, and others who care for horses to secure payment for debts.

The agister's lien was developed for custom feed lots and takes precedence over any other liens because livestock are considered perishable goods. The livestock must be fed, or would therefore perish, and the lien itself is against the livestock. This is different than the abandoned property law, which does not apply to livestock according to the Attorney General.

* There is another angle in which horses can be removed from the owner and that is under a court order for cruelty and/or

neglect. For horses to be removed from the owner action must be filed against the owner for cruelty. (Please see Chapter Nine, pages 75-80, Animal Abuse and Neglect laws for more details.)

Each state may have variations regarding the process of the agister's lien. The specifics regarding failure to correctly use the State Brand Board can be found under state statute and animal ownership or brand inspection laws. While the individuals employed by the state brand board are not in the business of prosecuting violators, they will prosecute owners who knowingly do not comply. Jail time and fines are listed among the penalties.

Collection of debts in all businesses and ventures can be very difficult and discouraging. Horse owners and business people would like to think that those they do business with are as honest as the horses they love. This is not the case, and a basic understanding of available collection procedures, and the problems that can be encountered, is helpful. Remember, in most cases, get professional help and advice BEFORE problems arise.

Chapter 6

Brand Inspection Laws & Horse Ownership

There are three times when a horse owner must contact the state brand board:

1. Whenever the horses (cattle, mules or donkeys) are transported over 75 miles within the state.

2. Any time horses (cattle, mules or donkeys) are transported across state lines.

3. Any time there is a change of ownership! Any change of title at all. And, both the buyer and the seller are equally liable for obtaining the brand inspection.

It is possible to get a permanent transportation card/brand inspection on a horse that is good for the duration of ownership. This permit is good anywhere in the continental United States. The exceptions are when transporting a horse to Alaska through Canada or to Hawaii. In those cases, it is necessary to get another permit the week of the transport.

Items to Remember

1. Inspection is required regardless of whether or not the animal is branded.

2. Inspection is required on all classes of stock (horses, cattle, mules, or donkeys). Registration papers or lack of registry does not exempt inspection.

3. The definition of a brand for the purposes of description is a permanent mark on the hide of an animal registered with any state as a livestock brand. (Tattoos are not brands.)

4. Inspection is required at the point of origin unless released by the local inspector.

Regulations

1. An inspection is required every time an animal is sold or purchased or when any change of ownership occurs, regardless of whether or not the animal is transported after or prior to the sale.

2. An inspection is required when livestock is to be transported over 75 miles totally within the boundaries of the state, with some exceptions. (Permanent brand cards are accepted.)

3. An inspection is required every time livestock leaves the state regardless of circumstances. (Permanent brand cards are accepted.)

4. Items 2 & 3 may be accomplished by the owner of the horse obtaining a "PERMANENT TRAVEL CARD." Brand inspectors welcome the opportunity to attend club/organization meetings and discussing brand inspection requirements or issue permanent travel cards.

5. Any time livestock is to be transported on a public road, proof of ownership should be avail-

able for inspection by the State Patrol, law enforcement or a brand inspector.

6. Animals being transported by a commercial hauler must have a "Bill of Lading" showing the point of origin, destination, number of head, color, sex, and the hot iron brands signed by the owner or agent of the stock.

7. Animals being transported by anyone other than the legal owner should have a letter or note from the owner authorizing that transport in conjunction with the inspection certificate.

8. Livestock crossing a state line must be accompanied by a current health certificate showing current vaccinations and a negative coggins test. Contact your local veterinarian or the state veterinarian office for specific information.

Out-of-State Livestock Purchases

Several states do not have an inspection law, and therefore, a certificate of inspection cannot be obtained. Contact the local livestock market to inquire about state regulations.

Always get a valid bill of sale and a health certificate when purchasing animals in non-inspection states.

The requirements of a legal bill of sale are:

- Seller's name,
- Buyer's name,
- Complete description of the animal(s) being purchased. Color, sex, breed, markings, registration numbers, and/or brands.
- Signature of seller,
- Signature of buyer, and

- Signature of a witness residing in the county where the transaction takes place.
- Having the bill of sale notarized is not necessary, but may be a good idea if a dispute arises.

The State Brand Board also has some jurisdiction over livestock after the owner has filed an Agister's Lien. (Please refer to Chapter Five, page 40, for details regarding the Agister's Lien.)

The individuals at the Brand Board stress that they are not in the business of prosecuting violators, they are there to help. However, they will prosecute owners who knowingly do not comply with the state's rules. Jail time and fines are listed among the penalties.

Source: **Gary Shoun**, Commissioner, State Brand Board of Colorado.

Chapter 7

Contracts

The universal rule to which there can be no reasonable exception is to get all agreements IN WRITING. In the horse business, or in any other business for that matter, agreements that are not in writing, oral contracts, are virtually impossible to enforce. In many instances, by statute, contracts that are not in writing are not enforceable. Examples of this include contracts for the sale of personal property over a certain sum of money (usually $500), and contracts for the sale of real estate.

This chapter will examine the elements of a proper contract, the need for contracts, and how to analyze and understand common contracts. Other than for the sake of example and instruction, no forms of contracts are included. Although there are some books on the market that purport to contain examples of "do-it-yourself" contracts, this book is an exception. I firmly believe that any business person should have competent professional assistance before entering into binding contracts that could effect his or her business. Thus, no "cure-all" or universal forms will be included in this book.

We all know that we no longer live in a simple and straight-forward time where "a person's word is their bond." Our world is both complex and legalistic, requiring formality and comprehensiveness in our contracts and agreements. The day of the handshake to seal the deal is gone. It has been replaced with the day of reducing all agreements to writing which contain the rights and obligations of all parties, and any other provisions that are agreeable to and are part of the transaction. Today, expert assistance is necessary in formulating, crafting, and interpreting many of the complex business transactions in the horse industry.

Even in situations involving less complex agreements or transactions, written contracts are vital. In sales of horses, boarding agreements, training contracts, and breeding transactions, written documentation is necessary for the protection of all parties.

Elements of a Contract

In law there is much discussion concerning the elements of a contract. By "elements" is meant those items which make up a proper and legally enforceable contract. Theses "elements" can also be called "requirements" and are:

FIRST: all contracts require an offer by one party who has the legal capacity and authority to make a contract

SECOND: acceptance of the offer by the other party

THIRD: a "consideration" is something you give (money, for instance) or do (such as provide a service) in return for something else

FOURTH: a meeting of the minds of the parties to the contract, and

FIFTH: reasonable certainty.

The five elements seem quite simple to understand and enforce, but they have been the subject of interpretation, controversy, dispute, and litigation for over 200 years. Since these "elements" are not as simple as they first appear, a more detailed discussion and analysis is probably appropriate.

An "offer" is legally defined as a proposal which, by its terms, is intended to become binding if the party to whom it is made accepts the offer. An offer can be one to buy or sell a horse for a certain sum of money, to trade a horse for another horse or something else of value, to board a horse for a certain sum of money per month, to train a horse for a specific purpose, or to breed the other party's mare to a particular stallion for a fee. There can be many other examples of "offers" in connection with horses.

"Legal Capacity and Authority to Make a Contract" refers mainly to age and mental state. In many states a minor (person under 18) is legally incapable of making a binding contract. A person who is insane, mentally retarded, or suffering the ravages of Alzheimer's disease, for instance, ordinarily lacks the mental ability to enter into a contract. This can also apply to an individual who is drunk or high on drugs at the time the contract is made, or who doesn't understand the implications of the contract. This is known as "mentally incompetent."

"Legal authority" to make a contract is important when a person is representing another. For example, if a trainer is asked to sell a horse while the owner is away on business and gives the trainer the necessary papers to transfer the horse, the trainer obtains the legal authority to make the sales contact on behalf of the owner. This would create a "principal" (the owner) "agent" (the trainer) relationship.

It is advised that you get the specifics of the agent's authority in writing. This paper may state the lowest price to be accepted and the terms to be considered. This document should also be notarized to make it more solid.

The next required element in a proper contract is "acceptance" which is simply saying "yes" to the offer. Agreeing to do, take, perform, or act on what has been offered is "acceptance." The law requires that acceptance of an offer must be of the identical terms of the offer and an agreement to be bound by the party who is accepting.

"Consideration," as a vital and necessary element of a contract, can be defined as a promise to do something, not to do something, or anything in between. It can be a promise to pay a certain sum of money, a promise to trade a certain item, forgiveness of an existing debt, or not to sue or make claim. In other words, almost any type or form of promise can satisfy the legal requirements of "consideration" in contracts.

"Meeting of the minds" simply means that all parties to the contract must understand and agree to the terms. The law requires that the parties know what they are getting into by entering into the contract. The rights, obligations, duties, and requirements of the contract must be known to, and agreed upon by all parties.

Finally, the fifth element of a proper contract is that of "certainty." A contract must be sufficiently definitive and complete in its terms so that the parties know and understand their respective rights and obligations. These "rights and obligations" cannot be estimates or guesses on what the parties are agreeing to do. The terms must be such that all parties know the material elements of the contract; for example, how much money will be paid, when it will be paid, where it will be paid, to whom it will be given, when the object or the contract will be delivered, where the delivery will occur, who will pay for transportation, etc. These are some examples of the requirements of "certainty" in contracts.

Without these five elements, preferably written on a dated sheet of paper, there is no contract. There is no specific requirement as to the form of the contract, but the elements must be properly included in the writing to make it an enforceable document.

Again, one should get professional advice before entering into any contract. The money spent on attorney's fees can be the greatest bargain any horse owner can receive. Not only can proper legal draftsmanship be obtained by using a qualified lawyer, but many of the statutory pitfalls and traps can be avoided.

Points to remember when writing a contract:

1. All contracts should have the date of creation or when it is signed. It should also have the dates events are to happen or when specifics of the contract take affect.

2. Body of the contract should include details which are to be understood by all parties. The terms of payments, warranties, descriptions of the services to be rendered or the animal being sold, and the default statement - what happens if the terms of the agreement are not met.

3. Signature(s) of the parties involved. This should reinforce that all parties have read and understand the agreement. This may include contact information, phone numbers and addresses.

Sales Contracts

Probably the most universal use of contracts or written documents for a horse owner is in the area of horse sales. Most states require written bills of sale for horses. By statute, for the transaction to be legal, most states require that the seller give the buyer a written "Bill of Sale" containing specific information about the animal being sold, including the horse's age, color, sex, markings, brands or tatoos. The buyer's and seller's respective addresses are required and, some states require a statement from a state brand inspector that the information of the Bill of Sale is accurate. In all cases, prospective buyers of horses should be aware of the particular state's requirements before purchasing the horse.

In addition to a Bill of Sale, most horse sales also involve a written sales agreement between buyer and seller. This document contains the five elements of a contract, discussed above, and serves as the agreement that controls the transaction. Since these written sales agreements are so common and important in horse transactions, a review of the areas covered by this contracts is important. Also, see the special section regarding auctions.

The first item to cover in the sales agreement is an identity of the parties. The full and correct address of the seller together with information concerning registration of the horse, where appropriate, should be included. The registration certificate, if any, should show the registered owner to be the same person as the seller, and the agreement, or the Bill of Sale, should provide for the execution and delivery of the certificate to the purchaser.

The full and correct name and address of the buyer should also be included in the sales agreement. If the horse will be financed or pledged as security for a debt (commonly, a portion of the purchase price of the animal), the exact name of the buyer together with any trade names should be included. For example if the buyer does business as "Blackmore Farm," the proper designation of the purchaser in the contract and any security agreements covering the horse would be: John Doe, d/b/a/ Blackmore Farm. Of course, if the buyer is a partnership or a corporation, the name of the entity would be indicated as the buyer.

The sales agreement should also contain a full and complete description of the horse, including the horse's name, year of birth, sex, color, sire, dam, and any appropriate breeding information. In the case of a broodmare, the stallion's name, date of last breeding, payment of stud fee, and any other appropriate data should be included.

Other important items to be covered in the sales agreement are the price of the horse and the terms of payment. The terms of the sale, whether cash or on installments must be fully covered by the contract. If the sale is for cash, the amount to be paid and when the payment is to be made must be clearly stated in the agreement. If the sale is on an installment basis, a number of subjects must be clearly spelled out in the contract including who will keep the horse until it is paid for.

The sales price must be stated, together with the amount of any down payment. The terms of the installment sale must be clearly stated, for example, the amount to be paid, whether payments will be monthly, quarterly, or annually; when each installment payment is due; where the payments are to be made; to whom they are paid; whether there is to be any security on the installment portion of the transaction; whether interest will be charged, and, if so, how much; and any other similar matters should be included.

The sales agreement should also contain a clear and accurate statement of all liens and encumbrances on the horse being sold. This is a very important provision to a buyer for obvious reasons; the purchaser wants to accurately know the purchase price being paid for the horse. The buyer does not want to be surprised later to discover that, in addition to the price paid to the seller, there is an additional amount owed to a secured creditor on the animal. If there is a lien or encumbrance on the horse, it must be disclosed to the buyer and dealt with in the sales agreement. In some cases, the buyer is assuming the debt on the animal and, if this is so, the contract should so state. If the amount of the debt on the horse is to be paid from the sale proceeds, this too should be addressed in the sales agreement, together with provisions ensuring that the buyer will receive the horse free of any encumbrances.

If the sale involves a granted or retained security interest in the horse, a number of issues must be addressed in the sales agreement and other necessary documents to protect the security interest. In the situation where there is a retained security interest in the horse, the Uniform Commercial Code governs how the security interest will be perfected to protect the seller (secured party) and the buyer (debtor). This is done by means of a Security Agreement and Financing Statement form, (UCC Form 1) that includes the following information: a description of the collateral (the horse); the full names and addresses of both the debtor and the secured party; a description of the horse; and the location of the horse until payment is completed. UCC Form 1 is filed and/or recorded with a designated state officer or agency to complete the security arrangement. Of course, if the debt is paid, the lien is released by written notification to the designated agency as provided by the law of the state of the transaction.

In addition to the sales agreement and UCC Form 1, in cases where there is a retained or granted security interest, the debtor also signs a promissory note containing the terms of the loan. All promissory notes must comply with the requirements of applicable negotiable instruments to be valid and enforceable. This simply means that the promissory note must be in writing, must be signed by the maker/debtor, must be for a certain sum of money, the debt must be paid on a certain date or within a certain time, and if interest is charged, it must be set forth. Any other conditions such as penalties for late payments, interest increases, or payment of attorney's fees on default, must also be stated in the note. If the promissory note is secured by a security agreement as previously discussed, this too must be stated in the note. It is important to know that a horse cannot be repossessed unless there has been a security interest retained or granted in the Bill of Sale or in the Security Agreement.

If the parties have agreed that mortality insurance on the horse will be required, the contract should so provide. The amount of insurance, payment of premium, conditions of insurance, and any other mutually agreed upon matters, should be included.

Although many people are by nature optimistic and feel that agreements will be fulfilled, reality shows that defaults are not infrequent. Therefore, the sales agreement should provide for remedies in the event of a default. Examples of defaults would include: a breach or failure to perform one or more terms of the agreement; failure to pay as provided; removal of the horse from the state without the consent of the creditor; bankruptcy of the debtor; an attempt to sell the horse before payment has been completed; or allowing the horse to be seized for the failure of the creditor to pay other debts. The parties to sales agreements should be aware of the possibility of defaults and address appropriate remedies.

For instance, in the case of a default caused by a breach of one of the terms of the agreement, the parties might include a provision in the contract that the breaching party has a certain period of time to cure the breach. Of course, in the case of a more serious default, the contract should contain protection for the innocent party and penalty provisions for the one breaching the agreement. These penalty provisions, which are principally financial in nature, if discussed early and included in the provisions of the sales agreement can certainly be deterrents to a party considering not performing his or her obligations. Anticipation of problems can go a very long way in preventing or, at least, minimizing their effect.

Included in most complete sales agreements are provisions for attorney fees and costs to be paid by parties who breach the terms of the contract. This can be one of the most effective deterrents to non-performance since attorney fees and costs can be very expensive and can, in many cases, be greater than the original amount in controversy.

In addition to provisions in sales agreements providing for attorney fees and costs, arbitration clauses are becoming quite common. An arbitration provision simply means that the parties agree to have any disputes or disagreements involving the contract, settled by arbitration rather than by lawsuit court. Arbitration is usually quicker and much less expensive than litigation, and is rapidly becoming the preferred method of dispute resolution.

Auctions contain the elements of a sales contract. When a person makes a bid at an auction, they are offering to buy the horse or tack for a certain price. The auction may contain a sealed bid called, "with reserve" meaning that the person selling the horse has set a limit on the minimum bid they will accept. Many auctions have rules requiring that the horse must sell to the highest bidder. This is legally called, "without reserve." Again, understand the requirements of the auction and those of the buyer and seller.

Express and Implied Warranties in Sales Contracts

In horse transactions a variety of disputes can arise leading to either litigation, arbitration, or some other form of dispute resolution. The most common are disputes involving breach of warranties under Article II of the Uniform Commercial Code. Since these controversies are so common, they should be reviewed in some detail.

The first of the two types of warranties is the "Express Warranty." Express warranties are statements, descriptions, or promises made by the seller to the buyer which relates to the horse or its uses, and which becomes a part of the basis for the transaction creating an express warranty that the horse shall conform to the statement, description, or promise. Some common examples of express warranties would include representations of the fitness of an animal for a particular purpose, e.g., "this horse would be a perfect hunter/jumper," or "this horse is a great race horse," or "your breeding program will be well served by this excellent broodmare."

The express warranties by a seller to a prospective buyer clearly become a basis for the transaction because the seller, in making the promise or statement, obviously knows of the buyer's plans or expectations for the horse, and is saying to the buyer expressly, this horse will meet your plans and expectations. If, after the transaction is completed, the horse does not live up to the promises or do as represented, controversy will surely result.

Another type of express warranty which can result in litigation, is that involving representations concerning the health of a horse. Most individuals in the horse industry are sophisticated enough to substitute contract provisions placing the duty on the buyer to obtain an examination by a veterinarian of the buyer's choosing, in place of an express warranty by the seller.

"Implied warranties" are also promises, statements, or descriptions which are not expressly included in the written agreement, but are made a part of the transaction merely by operation of law. Implied warranties include: a warranty that the horse is fit for the ordinary purpose for which horses are used, that the seller has the right to sell the horse, and of fitness for a particular purpose. The buyer is relying on the seller's judgment or skill in selecting the horse when questions about the horse are answered by the seller.

Since implied warranties are not specifically set out in the sales contract, they can become sources of controversy because of diverse interpretation. The saying, "there are two sides to every story," can take on a whole new meaning in trying to resolve cases involving claims of breaches of implied warranties. Again, fully and completely setting out the expectations of the parties in the written agreement can avoid many of these controversies. However, since implied warranties arise by operation of law, they are present in every transaction, and buyers and sellers alike should be aware of their existence and effect.

In addition to sales agreements, other common written contracts in the horse industry include breeding contracts, training agreements, and boarding agreements. Regardless of the type of contract or its subject matter, to be enforceable it must contain the elements of a contract previously discussed. However, specific types of contracts have their own unique areas that must be addressed.

Breeding Contracts

Breeding contracts should contain the following specific items:

- Identity of the mare and the stallion
- Location of the service
- Rebreeding rights, if any
- Statement of all charges incurred in the breeding and who will be responsible
- Veterinary services required, emergency treatment, physical examination, and certification of whether or not the mare is pregnant
- Provisions regarding a guaranty of live birth

The term "live foal" should clearly be defined. For example, as a foal that stands and nurses after foaling.

Breeding agreements become even more complex when the mare is to be bred using artificial insemination. The use of specific language regarding live births should cover proper collection of semen, amount to be delivered, transportation and other logistical complications. Additions to the contract may cover the presence of a veterinarian during insemination, and certification that only the designated mare was bred during this procedure.

Problems generally arise in breeding contracts regarding payments, such as how and when the stud fee will be paid. It should be understood by both parties that the owner of the stallion has the right to assert a breeder's lien if the fee is not paid. Having this written in the contract helps avoid surprises and fewer bad debts are incurred. Also, if there is to be any foal sharing, a separate agreement containing this arrangement should be made and signed by all parties.

Often, under the general category of "breeders contracts," are agreements whereby mares are leased for the purpose of breeding. As with all leases, the agreement should be in writing and contain clear statements of the agreed-upon terms and conditions. The lease should cover expenses, including veterinary services, transportation, risk of loss and mortality insurance. The agreement should contain a warranty of the one leasing the mare to the other party, that they own the horse or have the right to enter into the lease; and if the broodmare is secured, that they have a written release from the secured party authorizing the lease, and that any foals born would be free and clear of any liens or encumbrances. It is obvious that professional help is often needed in preparing comprehensive breeding contracts. There are many pitfalls to be avoided and an experienced attorney's services are often required to reach desired results. Breeding contracts are not for the inexperienced horse person, nor are they to be casually entered into.

Training Agreements

Training agreements, if properly drawn, can avoid many disagreements and controversies that can lead to tremendous expense. It is critical that the purpose and scope of the training is clearly understood by both parties, and that the contract reflects this. Agreements with trainers of racehorses are completely different than those with trainers for show horses. What the owner expects from the trainer must be set out in any agreement. Since training can be a very subjective matter, fairness to all parties (including the horse to be trained) requires a clear understanding of the abilities of the trainer and the expectations of the owner. Also, questions of costs, boarding fees, expenses, veterinary services, insurance and other similar issues should be addressed in the agreement.

If the agreement is for the training of a racehorse, very special and unique matters must be addressed. The contract must clearly state who has the right to make decisions concerning the training and the racing of the horse. Usually these decisions belong to the trainers, but some owners want the right to either make these decisions or, at least materially participate in the decision-making process. If this is not clearly understood and agreed in the contract between owner and trainer, severe controversy is almost assured.

Another critical area in race-training contracts is whether or not the trainer may run the horse in claiming races. If the owner would not approve of running the horse in a claiming race and the trainer goes ahead and runs it in a claiming race, problems can result. Obviously, any training agreement must define the rights and duties of the parties so that controversies and misunderstandings are avoided.

Boarding Contracts

The boarding of horses is a very common area where written agreements are important. Boarding contracts should include a statement of the costs, whether they are to be paid weekly or monthly, where the payments are to be made, what kind of facilities will be provided for the horse (for example, box stall, paddock, pasture, etc.),and whether veterinary services will be provided. Also, provisions concerning what to do if the horse becomes ill or injured, and related matters should be contained in the contract's terms.

Just as all other contracts, boarding contracts should be in writing, signed by all parties, and contain the rights and obligations of the signers. The owner of the boarding facility normally presents his boarding contract to the horse owner prior to the animal moving in. Sometimes the agreement is a printed or copied form regularly used by the stable for all boarders. On occasion, the contract is negotiated by the parties covering specific concerns and conditions that are present. In all cases, however, the agreement should clearly state what is being provided, how much money will be required, what will be furnished, what is not included, what happens if payments are late or not made, and what is to be done in the event of an emergency. Also, the document will probably discuss the question of any restrictions on the access to the facilities (including any time restrictions, forbidden areas for riding, use of facility for training, etc.). In short, all rules and regulations should be set out in the agreement, or in a written attachment thereto, and signed by the parties.

The principal goal of contracts is to describe, in writing, the understandings and agreements of the parties. A properly drafted contract attempts to avoid misunderstandings and controversies by clearly stating the respective rights and obligations of those who have entered into the transaction. It is an important business tool and has many applications including evidence in a trail or arbitration hearing, documentation for tax reasons, or for normal record keeping purposes. All too often people involved with horses forget that contracts are just as important in their business as in any other enterprise. This is a mistake and can be very costly. Conduct your horse activities as you would any other business. GET IT IN WRITING.

Chapter 8

Liability of Horsemen

The horse industry and horse people have felt the effects of the large number of claims and lawsuits by injured parties. In our society it now appears that whenever a person is injured (including all horse-related activities), the first thing to do is try to place the blame on someone else. We will not take the blame ourselves—it is always the "other guy's fault." (History has shown that this attitude sprang from abuses during the industrial revolution when certain protections were certainly needed.) As the frequency of lawsuits has increased, so has the novelty of the theories advanced to place the blame on others. This is certainly true in horse-related cases, and has led to vast increases in liability insurance premiums or, in some cases, total unavailability of insurance coverage.

The threat of lawsuits and the high cost of liability insurance has had the effect of creating a shortage of good facilities for the training of horses and riders. The horse industry has lost potential owners, riders, and participants in the business by this economically-forced shortage of proper facilities. If people are unable to follow their interest in horses and riding, the industry will be the loser.

This chapter discusses the traditional theories of liability that apply in the horse world and will concentrate on the more common situations where horse owners or keepers have been sued for harm allegedly done by the horse. The term "keepers" refers to those individuals who have control and/or custody of a horse or horses. This term includes trainers, breeders, livery stables, outfitters, etc.

The latter part of this chapter will cover legislation that has been enacted in a few states limiting the liability of the sponsors of all horse activities. These new laws have created a great deal of interest in horse circles, and attempts at enacting similar laws in other states are underway. Any person in the horse business or interested in horses in any way, should support these laws and work for their passage. In fact, owners of horses will need to become increasingly aware of laws that affect their business. Those include zoning laws, worker's compensation regulations, liability, taxation, and so many more.

Traditional Theories of Liability

Horses have, for the last 200 years, been classified by the law as domestic animals that are usually gentle creatures. They have long served the needs of man, at first as the primary method of travel, and in more recent times, as a great source of pleasure and recreation. However, when harm and injury caused by a horse occurs, the law holds the owner or keeper liable for the harm under two legal theories: strict liability and negligence.

STRICT LIABILITY is a legal theory that imposes liability on the owner or keeper of a horse who, because of prior experiences with the horse, knows that it has DANGEROUS PROPENSITIES and fails to take necessary or reasonable care to prevent injuries caused by the horse. Dangerous propensities can be described as the possibility to be dangerous because of prior actions. The knowledge of the keeper or owner of the horse of its habits and tendencies is key in determining liability. To understand the concept of "knowing a horse's dangerous propensities" it is helpful to examine how various courts have treated the question.

Recently, the Arizona Supreme Court held that a horse owner who had no prior knowledge of the horse's dangerous propensities was not liable for the injuries suffered by the plaintiff. A Florida Appellate Court has held that horses are not presumed to be dangerous. Ownership of the horse alone could not be the basis of liability. There must be evidence showing that the owner had knowledge of dangerous propensities for him to be held liable.

Courts in New York, Colorado and Indiana have followed the basic rule of law that actual knowledge of the horse's dangerous propensity is necessary to hold the owner liable. The New York case involved a claim by a woman who was injured when she fell from one of the defendant's horses at a riding stable. The court held that the defendant had failed to present sufficient evidence of notice of the horse's vicious propensities, and that the defendant could not rely on an implication of vicious propensities merely because the horse was a thoroughbred stallion. The United States District Court for Colorado, in a case prior to the Colorado statute limiting liability for equine activities, held that a horse that is known to bite or kick may have dangerous propensities, but a horse that has a tendency of expanding its chest (blowing up) while being saddled does not have an actionable dangerous propensity. The Indiana Court of Appeals stated in a recent decision that it is the owner or keeper's act or omission, not the horse's, which may lead to liability. However, the owner or keeper of the horse can breach his duty of care to the injured party only if he knew that the horse has a dangerous propensity.

Of course, not all courts have followed the "dangerous or vicious propensity" rule as uniformly as the higher courts. It seems that there has been a reluctance to follow the rule when the injured person is a child. The involvement of children in an accident has led to some rather interesting decisions. The North Carolina Supreme Court had to consider a case involving an injured nine-year old who had been kicked in the head by a horse after the child had crawled under a fence to enter the paddock. The court held that the vicious propensity rule did not apply in that or any other case where the injury was not caused by the viciousness of the animal. The North Carolina court ruled that the determinative issue of liability was not whether the owners knew of any vicious propensities, but instead whether they should have allowed the child to play with the horse when they knew he was inexperienced around horses.

A recent decision of the Court of Appeals of Kentucky also involved a young child crawling under a fence and being kicked in the head by a horse. The location of this incident made, in the court's opinion, the dangerous propensity rule inapplicable. In this case, the horse in question was kept in a fenced pasture in a residential neighborhood. The court stated that normally the keeper of a horse is not subject to liability unless the horse has known vicious propensities. But, the introduction of a herd of horses into a neighborhood populated by many children presents a different situation under the law.

The court held that the doctrine of "attractive nuisance" made the keeper of the horses liable. Under this legal doctrine, anyone who maintains upon his property any condition or thing which is dangerous to young children because they are too young and inexperienced to recognize the danger, and which may reasonably be expected to attract young children to the property, is under a duty to exercise reasonable care to protect them against the dangers of the attraction.

This case could, at least in Kentucky create difficulties for horse owners and keepers whose horses are kept near residential neighborhoods. In all states it should be remembered that the law attempts to especially protect young children from all perils. Horse owners and keepers must be very careful to protect young children, even if they trespass, from danger.

The doctrine of dangerous or vicious propensities is alive and well, and is somewhat protective to horse owners and keepers. However, it does not protect and apply to all situations. There is no substitute for taking reasonable precautions and having adequate liability insurance.

The other traditional theory of liability under which horse owners and keepers have been held liable is the theory of NEGLIGENCE. This theory means "a failure to do an act which a reasonably careful person would do, or the doing of an act which a reasonable person would not do, under the same or similar circumstances to protect others from injury, death, or damage." If an owner or keeper of a horse has knowledge of its dangerous propensities and fails to warn another person of them, this is negligent and liability results for injury or damage. This failure to warn, or failure to take measures or precautions to prevent injury by the horse, is "negligence."

The theory of negligence is broad and requires an analysis of the facts and circumstances of each case, to which is applied the definition of "negligence" to determine fault and the resulting liability. Of course "liability" means responsibility for the harm to another. The courts of North Carolina and Kentucky applied negligence theories rather than the vicious propensity rule in finding that the horsemen were liable to the injured children. The traditional theory of "negligence" is an ever present factor to be aware of in any horse operation. Vigilance, awareness, and proper risk management are the precautions necessary to avoid liability, or at least minimize its effect.

Statutes Limiting Liability for Horse Activities

Recognizing the damage to the horse industry, horse ownership and enjoyment caused by lawsuits, verdicts, and high insurance premiums, some state legislatures have passed statutes limiting liability for horse activities. The first state to enact this legislation was Washington, followed by Colorado. Attempts at passing a similar statute have failed in Virginia. However, horse associations and groups are attempting to introduce statutes limiting liability for horse activities in Michigan and several other states.

The Colorado statute is very typical of the laws which limit liability for horse activities. On July 1, 1990, the law entitled "Equine activities—legislative declaration—exemption from civil liability" became effective in Colorado. This statute exempts "equine activity sponsors, equine professional, or any other person (including corporations and partnerships) from liability for injury to or death of a participant "resulting from the inherent risks of equine activities." The Colorado Legislature stated in the bill that persons who participate in equine activities are exposed to some risk. However, the lawmakers found that the state and its citizens "derive numerous economic benefits" from such activities. The Legislature stated that its interest in passing the law was to limit the civil liability of persons involved in these equine activities.

The statute defines "engaging in equine activity" to mean "riding, training, assisting in medical treatment of, driving, or being a passenger upon an equine, whether mounted or unmounted, or any person assisting a participant or show-management."

The term "equine activity" covers six categories and includes:

First, "equine shows, fairs, competitions, performances, or parades" that involve horses (including, "dressage, hunter/jumper shows, grand prix jumping, 3-day events, combined training, rodeos, driving, pulling, cutting, polo, steeplechasing, English and western performance riding, endurance trail riding, western games, and hunting").

Second, equine training or teaching activities are included as "equine activities."

Boarding is the **third** category.

Fourth, riding, inspecting, or evaluating a horse belonging to another for the purpose of possibly purchasing the equine is included.

The **fifth** category is rides, trips, hunts, or any equine activity of any type that is sponsored by an equine activity sponsor.

The **sixth** activity is horse shoeing.

"Equine activity sponsors" are defined as anyone or any group that sponsors, organizes or provides facilities for an equine activity such as pony clubs, 4-H clubs, hunt clubs, riding clubs, schools, therapeutic riding programs, etc. "Operators, instructors, and promoters of equine facilities" including stables, clubhouses, pony rides, arenas, and fairs are also included under the category of "equine activity sponsors."

Under the statute, "equine professionals" are defined as persons engaged for compensation in instructing a participant or renting an equine to a participant for the purpose of riding, driving, or being a passenger upon the equine; or rental of equipment or fees to a participant.

"Inherent risks of equine activities" means "those dangers or conditions which are an integral part of equine activities, including but not limited to:

(I) the propensity of an equine to behave in ways that may result in injury, harm or death to persons around them:

(II) the unpredictability of an equine's reaction to such things as sounds, sudden movement, and unfamiliar objects, persons, or other animals;

(III) certain hazards such as surface and subsurface conditions;

(IV) collisions with other equine or objects;

(V) the potential of a participant to act in a negligent manner that may contribute to injury to the participant or others, such as failing to maintain control over the animal or not acting within his or her ability."

The statute defines "participant" as any person, amateur or professional, who engages in an equine activity, regardless of whether a fee is paid for the participation. This is as broad a definition as one can imagine.

The law, after making the definition of terms set forth above, provides that except for certain specific exceptions, equine activity sponsors, equine professionals, or any other person shall not be liable for an injury to or the death of a participant "resulting from the inherent risks of equine activity." Except for the specific situations in the statute, no participant or their representative shall make a claim against the equine activity sponsor, professional, or other person for injury, loss, damage or death.

The six specific situations where an equine professional, activity sponsor, or other person would be liable for a participant's injury or death are:

1. The statute does not apply to horse racing,
2. Knowingly providing faulty equipment or tack that causes injury or death.
3. It doesn't apply where the equine provider fails to make reasonable and prudent efforts to determine the participant's ability to safely manage the particular horse based on the participant's representation of his ability.
4. The statute does not apply to dangerous conditions on the equine provider's property for which warning signs have not been posted.
5. It does not apply if the equine provider commits an act or omission that constitutes willful and wanton disregard for the participant's safety, and the act or omission causes injury.
6. The law does not apply if the participant is intentionally injured.

To take advantage of the statute's protection, the law requires equine professionals to post and maintain notice signs in clearly visible locations where the equine professional or sponsor conducts the horse activity. The statute requires the following warning language on the sign:

> **WARNING**
>
> UNDER COLORADO LAW, AN EQUINE PROFESSIONAL IS NOT LIABLE FOR AN INJURY TO OR THE DEATH OF A PARTICIPANT IN EQUINE ACTIVITIES, RESULTING FROM THE INHERENT RISKS OF EQUINE ACTIVITIES, PURSUANT TO SECTION 13-21-119, COLORADO REVISED STATUTES.

The law requires that the warning notice be in black letters with a minimum of one inch in height.

The statute also requires that every written contract or document entered into by an equine professional for the "providing of professional services, instruction, or the rental of equipment or tack or an equine to participant, whether or not the contract involves equine activities on or off the location or site of the equine professional's business, shall contain in clearly readable print the warning notice."

A review of the statute's provisions makes it clear that the Colorado General Assembly intended to limit liability, suits and claims in horse activities. In general, its goal was met without damaging the legal rights of the public. Equine providers are still required to use prudence and care in the conduct of their activities. What the Legislature has added is accountability for one's own actions. Accountability has almost been forgotten in American law.

It is far too early to know whether or not this signals a trend, but individuals involved with horses can only continue to hope that the law is changing. Colorado and Washington horse people enjoy the protective benefits of these statutes. Other states have legislation of this type under consideration or about to be proposed. The opposition claims that these laws unduly favor a special interest—horse owners and keepers. The answer to this criticism is found in the statement of legislative intent in the Colorado statute as follows:

"The general assembly recognizes that persons who participate in equine activities may incur injuries as a result of the risks involved in such activities. The general assembly also finds that the state and its citizens derive numerous economic and personal benefits from such activities. It is, therefore, the intent of the general assembly to encourage equine activities by limiting the civil liability of those involved in such activities."

The actual wording of the Colorado statute may be acquired by writing the Colorado Horseman's Council or Pica Publishing.

Releases

Much has been written and discussed about the effect and desirability of Releases or Waivers in the horse business. In our society we all have been asked to sign waivers or releases—at the hospital, in renting an automobile, by our dentist, at the ski slopes, and before engaging in any activity where there is an element or risk of danger. The Release is viewed as being akin to an insurance policy—if a person signs a release, they are barred from pursuing a claim against the released party. This is, in many cases, simply not true.

To be binding and enforceable, the law requires that the person who signs the release fully know the actual facts, including the risks, and knowing these risks and facts, voluntarily elects to assume the risks in return for being allowed to participate in the activity. In the usual case where a potential rider is asked to sign a release before riding the horse, for the release to be effective, the prospective rider must either know or be advised of all the potential risks and misfortunes that he could encounter in riding the horse. Knowing all of these facts and risks, that rider goes ahead and, after fully reading the language of the release, signs it.

It is easy to see how difficult relying on releases can be in the horse industry where releases are often thrown in front of the riders immediately before the group mounts for the ride. As we will see, routine, wholesale releases can be ineffective.

While some releases are useless, well-drafted releases that are properly used and executed may protect horse businesses from negligence liability. The courts of a number of states have considered the effect of various releases. The decisions have universally examined the language of the particular release, the age of the signer, and the circumstances of the signing.

Recently, courts in California upheld a release signed by a lawyer as a condition to taking a riding lesson the lawyer was subsequently injured during the lesson. The lawyer claimed that the release violated public policy. However, the court disagreed and stated that it could find no constitutional or statutory authority that put horseback riding in the public interest. A similar result was reached by an Illinois court when it found that there was no public policy against enforcing riding stable releases. The court specifically found that the release was a binding contract in which the plaintiff had given up the attorney/riding student's right to sue.

A Michigan court held that a release signed by a guest at a resort ranch was valid and enforceable. The court noted that the language of the release clearly called the issue of liability to the signer's attention by stressing the dangerous aspects of horseback riding. However, a release signed by a fourteen-year-old riding student was voidable according to a Georgia court. This is why a well written release requests that a parent or guardian sign for anyone under 18 years of age.

In all of the cases above where releases where upheld, they had been signed by competent adults and were drafted by or with the assistance of attorneys. Too often releases are just common forms that are readily available and are too broad or vague to be enforceable. Horse businesses that are properly run should be aware that a matter as important as the avoidance of liability claims, should not be left to amateurs.

Competent professional help is a prudent investment in these matters.

Chapter 9

Animal Abuse and Neglect Laws

Virtually all states now have some form of law which protects animals from abuse and neglect. These laws are the result of a growing concern about the mistreatment of animals, including horses. Although there seems to be a universal recognition of the need for this legislation, there is disagreement over how the problem should be addressed.

There seems to be a growing battle between groups that have been called "animal rights" groups and other groups considered to have responsibility for harming animals. There is much confrontation and controversy between advocates of "animal rights" and those conducting rodeos, horse shows, endurance rides, hunter/jumper competitions, etc. The more extreme animal rights groups have conducted demonstrations and attempted to disrupt rodeos, horse shows, and other performances they deem to be exploitive of horses and other animals.

These demonstrations and other disruptions have led to the passage of the Animal Enterprise Protection Act of 1992 by Congress. This act makes it a federal offense to disrupt activities involving animals, including horse shows, rodeos, and other competitive animal events. This law became effective on August 26, 1992, and is intended to stop the increasing number of violent and unlawful acts by purported "animal rights" extremists groups against those conducting these animal activities.

The activities of extremists have, in the opinion of many, done serious harm to legitimate efforts to eliminate animal abuse and neglect. In the case of horses, most experts agree that in addition to strong anti-cruelty laws, there is a need for statutes that clearly address the question of what constitutes "proper care." This latter category involves proving a failure to give proper care which, without definition and standards, can be very difficult. Also, most cases involving horses fall in the area of not properly caring for animals rather than beating or openly abusing the equine. Horse groups and horse owners acknowledge the need for proper laws to avoid abuse and cruelty and are working for logical and enforceable statutes in these areas.

An example of positive legislation regarding animal abuse and neglect is the "Animal Protection Act" which was enacted in Colorado in 1990. In the language of the Act, its policy and intent is stated as follows:

"The general assembly hereby finds and declares that the protection of companion animals and livestock is a matter of statewide concern; and that it is the policy of this state that persons responsible for the care or custody of such animals be persons fit to adequately provide for the health and well-being of such animals."

The purpose of this legislation is to provide for the protection of mistreated, neglected, or abandoned animals, including horses. The Act provides for the seizure of animals and punishment of abusers.

The Colorado statute creates the Bureau of Animal Protection which is charged with its enforcement. Officers are trained to recognize improper care of horses and other animals. Quite often the symptoms of neglect are not readily apparent to the untrained observer. Through the efforts of animal rescue groups, veterinarians, and other horse experts, law enforcement officers are trained in what to look for in neglect cases. This makes the job of the officers easier and the rate of apprehension and successful prosecution of wrongdoers greater. Other states have enacted similar laws with varying approaches to enforcement.

Enacting and enforcing animal protection laws and laws protecting those legitimately using animals in competition are only one part of addressing the problem. The solution, in the opinion of most experts, lies in educating the public in the proper care and use of horses and other animals. This does not mean giving animals human personalities and emotions. What education is attempting to achieve in the areas of proper care and use, is how horses are constituted, their nutritional and medical needs, their tendencies, reactions, fears and pleasures, and related matters. If people understand the nature and needs of horses, they can better care for them and avoid unintentional abuse.

Those engaged in horse activities and horse ownership need to be aware of laws addressing cruelty and neglect, as well as efforts to educate the public about proper care and understanding of horses. Anti-cruelty and neglect legislation are indicative of the universal concern about animal welfare. This concern has spurred a variety of organizations to address the question. An example is the "Animal Welfare Code of Ethics" enacted and approved by the Colorado Cattlemen's Association in 1990. The Code's "Statement of Duty" contains an illustration of what seems to be happening in the responsible livestock industry, as follows:

"It is a livestock producer's duty to oppose inhumane treatment of livestock at any stage of the animal's life. Persons who willfully mistreat animals will not be tolerated in our business. We will provide any assistance necessary to the proper officials during the investigation and prosecution of individuals who abuse livestock under their care."

Although there has been substantial progress in the area of enacting anti-cruelty legislation, much remains to be done. Laws must define the standards of care to which horses need and to which they are entitled. (Standards of care differ widely among animal husbandry experts, animal rights groups, owners, and lawmakers making a true definition nearly impossible.) Laws must provide for penalties which are appropriate to punish wrongdoers and deter others from improper conduct towards horses. Forfeiture of the animals must be forced in extreme cases to prevent recurrence of the abuse. Adequate training of law enforcement personnel is necessary for proper enforcement of anti-cruelty laws. Finally, education of the public about the existence of these laws and proper methods of care of animals must be undertaken.

There are a number of fine organizations which are dedicated to saving and protecting horses. Although many similar organizations exist throughout the country, the following is a list of protective organizations whose emphasis is nationwide:

American Horse Protection Association, Department HI, 1000 29th Street NW, Suite T-100, Washington, D.C. 20007, (202) 965-0500

Hooved Animal Humane Society, 10804 McConnell Road, Woodstock, IL 60098-0400, (616) 245-8517

Large Animal Protection Society, P.O. 223, Parkersburg, PA 19365,

These organizations, together with local horse rescue groups, are worthy of the support, both personal and financial, of horse owners. In addition to political lobbying and monetary gifts, humane organizations need volunteers.

Organizations Set Rules To Protect Animals

Organizations are taking steps to prevent cruelty by developing rules and now these rules are standing up to the test of the courts. Associations in every facet of the horse industry have developed rules and tests to protect riders, horses and animals in competition. Show horses undergo testing for drug abuse, judges check for humane curb straps and other equipment, but now the associations are going further.

The Professional Rodeo Cowboys Association (PRCA) has approved a fine of $100 against any cowboy who "jerks down" a calf during calf roping. A jerk down occurs when a calf roper flips a calf on its head or back after it is roped. This fine will help prevent potential injuries to the calves. The fine is instituted at the discretion of the management of each rodeo.

What is more important than just setting rules, is that the courts are standing behind these organizations when they are taken to court. Examine the following case.

Higginson v. American Quarter Horse Association begins with a quarter horse stallion named Silver Inspiration, who was found to have had his tail surgically altered. This violated a new rule of the AQHA's tail testing program. The owner, John Higginson of Sunland, California, appeared before the AQHA's Executive Committee, who revoked the horse's show privileges, suspended Higginson from participation in AQHA approved shows for 90 days and fined him $500.

Twice the owner requested the reinstatement of show privileges and then filed a case against the AQHA asking for "monetary damages for alleged injury to his reputation as a trainer and loss of income to his breeding program with Silver Inspiration, mandatory reinstatement of the stallion's show privileges, and attorney fees."

On August 25, 1992, the Texas court decided in favor of the American Quarter Horse Association and against Higginson and ruled that he reimburse the AQHA for its attorney's fees in defending the case.

Horsemen and organizations must continue their efforts to ensure that the animals receive proper care and are free from abuse and neglect.

Chapter 10

Buying Horse Property

One of the most common areas of legal problems for horse owners involves purchasing horse property. An ideal goal of horse owners is to have a place where they can live, keep their horses, ride and enjoy a "country lifestyle." Prospective purchasers spend a great deal of time locating what appears to be suitable property. Often, real estate agents are consulted to assist in the search for that "perfect piece of ground." As various properties are seen, the excitement can grow and people can be consumed by their plans and dreams. This is often wonderful but, unless the enthusiasm is tempered with reason and judgement, great trouble can lie ahead.

A great deal of research and investigation is necessary by any prospective buyer after what appears to be the perfect property is found. There are many physical, legal, practical, and political factors that must be investigated before buying any horse property. Too often prospective purchasers think that a parcel of real estate appears to be rural or agricultural, that it would be suitable for maintaining horses and using it accordingly. Wrong! We all know that looks can be deceiving and this is certainly true with real estate. As stated above, many factors must be thoroughly investigated before buying the ground.

Ask About Zoning

The first question that must be asked is "What is the ZONING of the real estate in question?" How property is zoned determines how it can be used. Zoning classifications are now quite common in rural areas. Often, entire counties are zoned to enable planned uses and to control growth and development. Many components are included in zoning, including whether horses or livestock may be kept, maintained and used on the particular property. In addition, there are often restrictions on the number of horses per acre or on each lot, as well as requirements for barns, corrals, pastures, weed controls, water, and other restrictions or requirements. Especially in areas that are near residential development, numerous and sometimes rather unreasonable requirements on the keeping of horses, make even the most attractive property unsuitable for having horses.

How do you find out about the zoning on a specific piece of property? The most reliable method of determining the zone classification of property is to go directly to the county or city zoning department or authority. Usually the county department will be very helpful, not only in giving accurate information on the zoning, but will also be able to tell prospective purchasers of the restrictions or prohibitions they would face under the applicable zoning ordinance for their planned horse facility. Copies of the zoning laws containing the requirements and restrictions are also available from the department. Armed with this information, the horse owner can be a more informed buyer, or non-buyer, as the case may be.

Of course, real estate agents can also be a good source of information on zoning. However, the better practice is to either go to the zoning department yourself and get the information directly from those persons who enforce the zoning laws. While a real estate agent might know the zoning classification of the land, technical requirements and restrictions that could have an adverse effect on the keeping of horses, might be out of the agent's knowledge or understanding. Get the information on zoning straight from "the horse's mouth."

In addition to zoning, a prospective purchaser must determine if there are any restrictive covenants are rules that effect the property. "Restrictive" or "protective" covenants that affect the property which must be met for its proper use. If an owner of the land does not follow the covenants, legal action and other penalties can follow. Accurate copies of restrictive covenants are available from title insurance companies. Often it is wise to obtain legal counsel to review and interpret the covenants and advise on their effect. Generally, only subdivided and platted subdivisions contain protective covenants, however, all property should be checked to see if they affect the subject property.

Title insurance companies can be used to determine what encumbrances, if any, are against the property. Also, title commitments can reveal other problems with the property such as tax liens, lis pendens (notification that the title to the property is disputed), judgement liens, and other similar matters. Title commitments from title insurance companies are a relatively inexpensive, but very important resource for a buyer of property to know a great deal about the legal status and title to the real estate.

Suitability for Horses

The next question that requires investigation involves whether or not the property is suitable for horses. The area of "suitability" is very broad and includes: area, pasture, environmental concerns, water, weeds, latent dangerous conditions or defects, and political concerns. These questions contain both legal and practical concerns and often require obtaining professional help in gathering the data necessary for a proper decision.

Too often horse owners underestimate the amount of ground necessary to properly maintain horses. At least in the western United States, very few tracts of land can provide adequate feed for horses without supplement. Newer horse owners usually have problems properly determining the size of land necessary for the horse. Expert advice is often necessary in determining the proper size and location for the horse operation even for experienced horse people. This information can be obtained from local extension offices and special books written for horsemen regarding landplanning and barn building. Also, never be afraid to ask others for what they have done, or what they have had problems with.

Environmental Concerns

Environmental concerns present a virtual mine field for land owners. If a person buys a parcel of ground that contains toxic waste or substances that are deemed unsafe by the Environmental Protection Agency (EPA), under federal law, the purchaser can be liable for clean-up costs. This liability attaches to the owner of the land, regardless of whether or not the owner had anything to do with creating the environmental problem.

We hear of these problems in urban areas where land is bought that formerly was the site of an industrial business. Why would this be any concern to a horse owner looking for a nice piece of rural property? The answer is simply that due to formerly common practices that were followed in the country, serious environmental problems are all too common. For example, in the past many farmers disposed of oil, commercial fertilizer residue, pesticide left overs, etc. simply by pouring them on what they considered to be less valuable ground. These substances do not simply vanish; they saturate the ground, leech into groundwater, and contaminate all that they contact. This is how some "Super Fund Sites" have been created that will cost millions of dollars to clean-up. Also, most rural areas had an area for dumping trash. These too often contain toxic materials that have been abandoned for years and require large sums of money for cleanup.

In some areas and under certain laws, a defense of being an "innocent purchaser" might be of some help. However, the cost and trouble involved in these environmental matters can be considerable even if the buyer is "innocent." Investigation in this area requires expert assistance. In some instances a complete "environmental audit" of the real estate is necessary to determine whether it is free from these concerns. The best course available to a prospective purchaser is to obtain expert advice and assistance before signing the contract. Professionals will discover and verify the former use(s) of the land. Abstracts and other public records will be searched to determine prior ownership. An effort will usually be made to discover what is referred to as "local knowledge" about the particular tract of land--to find out about the "skeletons in the closet." In short, experts, whether attorneys or engineers, will attempt to discover problems that are present on the land. The advice of these professionals should be strictly followed to prevent the nightmare of environmental problems.

Another area of concern and investigation, especially in the western United States, is that of water. In semiarid locales, water use and consumption are strictly regulated. There are many rural or rural-appearing properties that are wholly unsuitable for horses because of either the unavailability of water or because water on the property cannot be used for livestock. In many states household use of water does not allow the watering of horses or other large animals. Obviously, a property without usable water is totally unsuitable for use as a horse property. The water question can easily be determined by contacting local authorities (e.g. zoning, county agents, utilities. etc.) Water quality must also be investigated well in advance of purchasing property.

Closely associated with water are questions of pollution and groundwater contamination. Equine manure cannot contribute to or cause either groundwater contamination or surface runoff pollution. Also, manure must not cause air pollution or noxious conditions such as flies or other insects that adversely affect the surrounding area. Other concerns include parasite and rodent control, together with control of dust, odors and pesticide drift. If septic systems are either in place or are to be constructed, a potential purchaser must be aware of what tests and inspections are required by local health and/or building authorities. Horse owners must be sensitive to these problems and take appropriate precautions to comply with all applicable state and local health regulations. Again, a potential purchaser should check with local authorities to find out about all regulations that affect the use, stabling and maintenance of horses in the area. Prior knowledge can avoid costly and serious mistakes.

As previously discussed, that "dream place in the country" can be a nightmare. Even the most desirable-appearing property can be wholly unsuitable as a horse property. Research, professional assistance, and common sense can go a long way in avoiding possible problems. Plan ahead, investigate, research, and get the necessary professional help before you purchase the property. Your dreams and goals can be realized if you know what you are getting, and it meets your needs.

Chapter 11

Products Liability

A horse owner buys a 50 pound bag of horse feed. Within hours of feeding it to his horse, the animal is either very sick or dead. Another horseman purchases medicine for his horse which is designed for the prevention of a specific disease or condition. After administering it to the animal, it either dies or becomes violently ill. Finally, a horse owner buys new tack for her horse, including a new cinch. After installing the cinch on her saddle, while riding, it breaks and she is injured.

All of these incidents involve "product liability" law which attempts, in proper cases, to compensate the victim for his or her losses by assessing damages against the company that produced the defective product. Common product defects include: faulty packaging, inadequate warnings of possible dangers from the product, design flaws, and manufacturing defects. Usually, in most personal injury cases or matters involving damage to property, the claimant must show that the injuries occurred because of someone else's negligence. However, in product liability cases, the law of most states imposes "strict liability" on the manufacturer and, sometimes on the seller, of the defective product. This simply means that it is not necessary for the injured party to show negligence, but only that the injury was caused by a product that was in some way defective.

Common Defenses

Of course, manufacturers are given several defenses to product liability suits and claims. These defenses include the following:

1. That the person bringing the suit or claim was not really injured by the product.

2. The statute of limitations has expired. In all matters, victims have only a limited time in which to bring suit for damages, usually one or two years from the time the injury occurred, was discovered, or when the product was sold to the first purchaser (not necessarily to the injured party). After this time period expires, no suit can be brought against the manufacturer.

3. The product was altered in some unforeseeable way after it left the manufacturer's factory. If a customer, seller or shipper alters the product, and that alteration causes or contributes to the injury, the manufacturer may not be liable.

4. The injured party assumed the risk of using a dangerous product. Some products are inherently dangerous and a person can be hurt if they are careless.

5. The danger of the product was so obvious that special warnings were not needed. This defense is not as successful as some of the others under strict liability law. Generally manufacturers give warnings with almost all products, even the most obviously dangerous.

6. The product was used in an unforeseeable way by the victim. An example of this defense would be trying to use a cinch as a tow rope.

Protect Your Rights

It is important for the horseowner to know what to do when an injury occurs because of a defective product. There are several steps that should be taken after the injury to protect the injured party's rights and preserve a complete factual record for future use. The most important thing to remember is to KEEP THE EVIDENCE. Whatever is left of the product should be gathered up and kept in a safe place. This is critical to preserve a link in the chain of evidence that goes directly to the question of what caused the injury and why. Often, product liability cases involve later testing of what is left of the product. Remember to keep the evidence.

Consult with a lawyer as soon as possible for advice and counsel. Not all attorneys handle product liability cases, but consulting with your lawyer will often result in a reference to a specialist in the field.

Gather all the facts. Note the manufacturer's name, the model of the product, any serial number, keep sales receipts, and retain any packing or instructions. Write exactly when and where the incident occurred and under what circumstances. List the names, addresses and telephone numbers of all witnesses to the incident, including all doctors and hospitals or veterinarians who treated the injured party or horses.

Product liability cases can occur without warning. Although they are fortunately not too common, they do happen. It is always best to be aware of the potential danger of a product and to know what to do if you are a victim.

Chapter 12

Laws Governing Horse Trailering

A common part of horse ownership and use is trailering the horse(s) to the veterinarian, horse shows, rodeos, trails, polo matches, and other similar places. The ownership and use of horse trailers is very common in the equine world. Until recently, a horse owner did not have to have any special license to haul his horses from place to place, unless a great number of horses necessitated the use of a large van or semi-trailer. On October 26, 1986, Congress passed the Commercial Motor Vehicle Safety Act (the Act). This Act went into effect on April 1, 1992 and every horse owner must be aware of the effect of these new laws on their horse trailering activities.

Goal & History of the Commercial Motor Vehicle Safety Act

The goal of the Act is to improve highway safety by ensuring that drivers of large trucks and busses are qualified to operate those vehicles on the highway. This Act provides that each state retain the right to issue driver's licenses, but establishes minimum national standards which each state must meet when licensing the driver of larger vehicles, known as, Commercial Motor Vehicle (CMV) drivers.

In years past, many of the 50 states did not require the drivers of large busses or vehicles to have any special training, thus creating inconsistent rules throughout the nation. This Act is a combined effort to change those inconsistencies. The Act makes it illegal to hold more than one license at a time. By only holding one driver's license, drivers with violations or convictions will not be able to spread those violations over several states. A second point of clarification is to set standards to adopt testing and licensing standards for all truck and bus drivers. This will ensure that all drivers are able to operate the type of vehicle he plans to operate.

New Rules to Drive By

With the enactment of the Commercial Vehicle Safety Act of 1986, and the regulations thereunder imposed by the Federal Highway Administration, new and unfamiliar requirements are imposed on the hauling of horses.

Under these new laws, a driver of a rig as small as a six-horse gooseneck trailer pulled by a one-ton pickup (of a loaded gross vehicle weight exceeding 26,000 pounds) is now required to get a Commercial Driver's License (a.k.a. CDL). The CDL is still obtained from the state's motor vehicle bureau, but now requires a number of additional requirements.

- A written test and a driving skills test is required.
- The driving test has to be taken in the type of vehicle the applicant expects to use in hauling horses.
- In addition, a detailed background check of each applicant is necessary, and strict reporting of accidents, traffic convictions, and other similar matters is required.
- An important new requirement being imposed on drivers is a medical certificate verifying that the driver has the physical ability to operate the vehicle. This medical certificate must be carried by the driver, along with his commercial driver's license.
- Another new legal requirement is that the driver must now carry a log book to record all trips of over 100 miles from his place of residence.

- Finally, the new federal laws have strict inspection requirements and certifications for commercial vehicles.

Each State to Provide Final Regulations/Exemptions

Federal regulations are only minimum requirements and each state may enact further safety standards. Each state even has the option to "grandfather" drivers with good driving records from the skills test. That is, if they meet special criteria set up by the federal government.

States are able to choose to exempt drivers from having to get a commercial driver's license who only transport their own horses for nonbusiness purposes.

Drivers of farm vehicles may also be excluded from the CDL requirements. Farmers are subject to the Federal Motor Carriers Safety Regulations because they often carry hazardous materials like pesticides. Horsemen often transport hay, straw or shavings, all of which are extremely flammable and are considered hazardous. It is the driver's responsibility to understand the safety standards adopted by their state and have the appropriate insurance coverage. It would be advisable to question whether your state considers your type of equine business to be a farming activity.

The Federal Motor Carrier Safety Regulations probably effect more horse owners than the new CDL requirements. These are not new requirements and apply to vehicles used in interstate commerce, which have a gross weight of over 10,000 pounds and the transportation is "in furtherance of a business enterprise." The hobby horse owner may want a clearer definition regarding whether he is engaged in "a hobby" or "interstate commerce."

Making all of this even more confusing is that many states have additional and more stringent requirements than the federal regulations. Current information may be obtained from each state department of motor vehicles.

Because of these new requirements and the states' implementation of these new laws, smaller truck and trailer rigs may be regulated as well. It could happen that an owner of a two horse trailer with a 1/2 ton truck pickup is subject to some Federal Motor Carrier Safety Regulations. The driver may not be required to have a commercial driver's license, however they must carry both a health card and a log book when operating the vehicle.

Please note, that the owner of the trucks, trailers and horses employing someone else to do the driving is the person responsible for living up to the regulations

A very important requirement of the law is that now ALL trucks and trailers must now stop at weigh scales. This requirement is now enforced by the Federal Department of Transportation, and is no longer controlled by the states. It should also be noted that the individual states have not lost all of their regulatory powers over trucks and trailers. Most state's laws in this area are still in effect and will be enforced. The stated goal of these federal interstate trucking laws is to improve highway safety in conjunction with existing state laws. It is important for all drivers of horse trailers or vans to be fully aware of and in compliance with these laws. Vigorous enforcement of these new laws has been promised by the Department of Transportation and horse owners should be aware of their requirements.

The Federal penalty to a driver who violates this provision is a civil penalty of up to $2,500 or, in aggravated cases, criminal penalties of up to $5,000 in fines, or up to 90 days in prison, or both. An employer is also subject to these penalties, if he uses a driver to operate a commercial motor vehicle (CMV) without proper license.

An informed representative from your State Office of Motor Vehicles or the Office of Motor Carriers could be an excellent speaker for your class, club or organization. Check with the government pages in your local phone directory or check with Table A at the end of this chapter to locate the appropriate phone numbers. Call and request the specific requirements of your state regarding the driving of horse trailers.

The American Horse Council provides three brochures entitled: "*How Federal Motor Carrier Safety Regulations Affect Horse Trailers,*" *The Commercial Driver's License Program*" and " *Office of Motor Carriers Division Offices.*" All are prepared by the Federal Highway Administration. Send $2 to AHC at 1700 K St. N.W., #300, Washington, DC 20006-3805 to order the brochures.

Table A

Office of Motor Carriers Division Offices

Alabama	(205) 223-7244
Alaska	(907) 271-4068
Arizona	(602) 379-3646
Arkansas	(501) 324-5050
California	(916) 551-1300
Colorado	(303) 969-6748
Connecticut	(203) 240-3708
Delaware	(302) 734-5323
District of Columbia	(202) 523-0178
Florida	(904) 681-7462
Georgia	(404) 347-4966
Hawaii	(808) 541-2700
Idaho	(208) 334-1842
Illinois	(217) 492-4602
Indiana	(317) 226-7474
Iowa	(515) 233-1775
Kansas	(913) 267-7288
Kentucky	(502) 227-7321
Louisiana	(504) 389-0390
Maine	(207) 622-8358
Maryland	(301) 962-2889
Massachusetts	(617) 494-2770
Michigan	(517) 377-1866

Minnesota	(612) 290-3260
Mississippi	(601) 965-4219
Missouri	(314) 636-3246
Montana	(406) 449-5224
Nebraska	(402) 437-5521
Nevada	(702) 784-5681
New Hampshire	(603) 225-1626
New Jersey	(609) 989-2276
New Mexico	(505) 764-6788
New York	(518) 472-6483
North Carolina	(919) 856-4378
North Dakota	(701) 250-4346
Ohio	(614) 469-5657
Oklahoma	(405) 231-4607
Oregon	(503) 399-5775
Pennsylvania	(717) 782-4443
Rhode Island	(401) 528-4578
South Carolina	(803) 765-5414
South Dakota	(605) 224-8202
Tennessee	(615) 736-5951
Texas	(512) 482-5474
Utah	(802) 828-4480
Virginia	(804) 771-2386
Washington	(206) 753-9875
West Virginia	(304) 347-5935
Wisconsin	(608) 264-5215
Wyoming	(307) 772-2305

Current as of June 1992

Chapter 13

Estate Planning for Horse Owners

Horse ownership brings with it many responsibilities. Everyone knows about the need to properly care for their horses to feed them, provide adequate water, keep them in safe and secure surroundings, and provide veterinary care. However, many horse owners ignore the need to consider their horses when planning their estate.

For most people, estate planning means planning for our death and the distribution of the property we have accumulated. The most important tool used in the distribution of one's property is a properly drawn will.

This chapter is not intended to be a detailed discussion or analysis of estate planning, but is meant to share some information and suggestions that will help horse owners properly provide for the care and disposition of any horse(s) that are a part of their estate.

According to the law, and for the purposes of determining assets, horses are considered personal property. (Please note however, animals are living creatures needing care and feeding, making them unlike other personal property.) When a person dies, all of his assets become part of his estate. If the person has made a valid will prior to his death, the provisions of the will dictate how his or her personal property will be divided, distributed and disposed of.

A business, including a horse-related business, is considered an important part of your estate. Businesses require special planning. This will be discussed later.

What Happens If You Don't Plan

If you die without a will or other estate planning tool (such as a living trust), your property will be distributed according to the laws of "intestate succession" of the state where you were living at the time of your death. One who dies with a will is legally described as dying in, "testate." On the other hand, a person who dies without having made a will, dies "intestate." Rather than directing how the property is distributed and administered, an intestate estate is distributed according to a statutory scheme of the state where the decedent resided. As a lawyer, I strongly advise everyone to have a will. It is easy, relatively inexpensive, and can save family and friends a great deal of trouble later.

Every horse-owner should have a will that, in addition to the other necessary provisions concerning the distribution of his or her property, should provide for the immediate care of the horses upon the death of the owner. Unlike inanimate objects that are owned by the deceased, horses require uninterrupted care.

One of the important provisions in every will is the selection of a Personal Representative (sometimes called "Executor" or "Executrix") who is a person or institution charged with carrying out the wishes and directions in the will. Horse owners should select a Personal Representative who is both able and willing to carry out the directives relating to the horses that are expressed in the will.

Thoughtful consideration should be given on the question of suitable disposition of the horses in the will. Who does the horse owner want to receive the horses? Is the recipient able to care for the horses? Does the recipient want the horses? What is in the best interest of the horses? If the recipient cannot receive the horses, what alternative plan would be best for their proper disposition?

Occasionally, a newspaper article appears in which an eccentric millionaire leaves money or property to a favorite animal. "Is this legal?" you may ask. No. The gift of money or property is invalid in the eyes of the court. This is because animals are unable to hold legal title to a house, car or other personal property, much less open a bank account. It is advisable to appoint a guardian or gift money to a horse rescue organization.

Some people have asked that upon their death their horse, or other beloved pet, be put to sleep. At one time these provisions were followed without question. However, animal protection groups has successfully challenged this practice.

In my practice, I advise my clients to prepare a separate written letter for use by the Personal Representative or custodian of the horses relating to their care. In this letter I suggest that they include the current name, address and telephone number of their veterinarian; the health record of the horses; and any special instructions concerning the feeding or care of the horses.

There are many pitfalls involved in estate planning which have led to many lawyers, and nonlawyers, specializing in estate planning. Horse owners should consult a competent attorney to prepare their will and should feel comfortable with the guidance this person provides. Horse owners should take extra care in providing as much information as possible to the attorney during this process. Think ahead, and remember to provide for your horses in your estate.

Chapter 14

Insurance Considerations

Selecting the Right Agent

A capable insurance agent should be considered a part of any successful equine business. As with any other member of your inside team, you will want to interview this person to ensure that his knowledge is up-to-date and his products fit your situation. Some good questions to ask include: "Do you have any advanced degrees or training?" "As an agent, how many companies do you represent or policies are you able to offer us for our specific needs?" "How many horse-related businesses or individuals have you written contracts for this year / during your career?" "How many years of experience do you have writing this type of policy?" A good rule of thumb is to select an agent who accounts one-fourth of his business to writing horse-related policies.

When comparison shopping in this manner, remember to tell each agent the same information. You may even want to have your questions written down and write down each prospective agent's answers. Make sure you are comparing prices for the same service and coverage. An indication of a good agent will be his ability to ask you specific questions about your operation and that he will be able to offer some options. The best option for you should be affordable and offer excellent protection of your investments.

There are state and national tests insurance brokers and agents must take to sell insurance within the state. It is a growing trend for the state insurance commission, in some states, to require a specific number of hours of higher education in addition to passing the state and federal exams. Requiring some type of recertification education is also becoming popular. In addition to these tests, agents can earn special designations or degrees by taking exams provided by universities or organizations interested in promoting the profession. By passing these additional exams, the agent/broker may add initials behind their names like, CIC, CPCU, or IIA.

Once the professional expertise of an insurance broker is determined, it is important to determine that the insurance company itself is stable. Even after the agent tells you that it is a great company and the paperwork looks impressive you can check for yourself at your local library. The publications for reference include: *Best's Insurance Reports, Standard & Poor's, Moody's Investor Services* and *Duff & Phelps*.

Make sure the insurance company is licensed in the state in which you reside. The state insurance commissioner, superintendent or director will be able to inform you of the status of the company in your state. In some states you will want to look under regulatory agencies in the "blue" or government pages of your phone book. Making a few calls will protect you, the insured party, in the event the insurance company ceases operation.

If you still want to know more about your insurance agent, you can contact the National Association of Professional Insurance Agents or Independent Insurance Agents of America. Standard and Poor's will send you, free of charge, a list of rated insurance companies. Call Standard & Poor's Insurance Rating Information Department at (212) 208-1527 and be prepared to hold while a representative picks up your call.

It is of the utmost importance that the agent has a working knowledge of the horse industry and listens to your specific needs. Determining what types of insurance the broker/agent has had experience with is important as well as his concentrated experience in insuring similar types of facilities or activities. Quality of coverage, not price, should be the determining factor after all bids have been reviewed.

There are several forms of insurance coverage which apply specifically to the horse industry. The six basic types of coverage are: 1. mortality, 2. loss of use, 3. surgical/major medical, 4. liability, 5. property (i.e. tack) and 6. Auto insurance and coverage for the drivers. Liability can even be divided between farm operations liability and competition liability. (Competition liability is covered indepth in Chapter Eight, Liability of Horsemen; and Product Liability is covered in Chapter Eleven.) Since mortality insurance has many of the elements of all equine insurance, let's begin with this subject.

Examining Equine Mortality Insurance

"Mortality insurance" is another name for life insurance for horses. Most mortality policies cover death by sickness or accident. It also covers theft. The average rate may range from 3% to 6% or the total value of the horse. Avoid "limited mortality" forms of coverage because they only cover death due to accidents and not sickness.

Horsemen often have mortality insurance on their horses, but make the common mistake of applying what they know about human life insurance to the policies on their horses. This can create problems and misunderstandings because of the differences between the two types of policies. Too often horsemen do not understand the terms and limits of their equine mortality insurance.

Insurance policies are contracts. In return for the premium, the company agrees to provide certain coverage. In the case of equine mortality insurance, it covers for the death of the horse during the policy period (usually one year).

The policy contains conditions that must be strictly followed by the insured to keep the coverage in effect. The most common condition in equine insurance is the obligation to give written notice to the insurance company of any accident, illness or disease suffered by the covered horse. Failure to comply with this requirement can void the coverage.

When this contract is entered into you will be given a toll free phone number to call in the event the horse becomes sick or needs to be put down. This is a very important number you should be able to call 24-hours a day. Also, an agent should give you a binder of the policy immediately. This can be done by fax if you come to an agreement on the phone. Beware of agents who speak in general terms or are vague, using statements like, "Don't worry that's all covered." or "I'll write in all the details at the office."

In addition to knowledge of the policy conditions, the owners must be aware of the exclusions from coverage in the policy.

Common exclusions in equine mortality insurance policies include:

- Intentional slaughter of the covered horse unless the insurer has agreed in the terms of the policy that a veterinarian can provide a certificate that the destruction was necessary to prevent inhumane suffering.
- In the event of poisoning, it must be proven to be accidental.
- Theft or escape of the horse is often excluded unless it is specifically covered in the policy. In the case of theft coverage, policies usually require immediate notice of the loss to law enforcement agencies and to the insurer. (Mysterious disappearances are not covered.)
- The death of the covered horse caused by certain surgery is often excluded unless it was done by a qualified veterinarian; was certified by the vet to be

necessary because of accident, illness or disease; and was done to save the horse's life.

Over the years, disputes involving equine mortality insurance have led to extensive litigation. Courts have been asked to resolve controversies over the actual value of the deceased horse when:

- The promptness and adequacy of the notice to the insurance company is questionable,
- the horse was euthanized,
- fraud may be involved, or
- loss of use or disability cases.

When the controversy involves the value of the horse, the question is usually whether the horse was covered for ACTUAL VALUE or AGREEDED VALUE. This amount, of course, should not exceed the insurance policy's limits on that particular horse.

Insured values are usually based on the purchase price. If homebred, the company will usually insure to twice the stud fee. Increased values require justification of value such as training fees paid, breeding records, show records, appraisals, and must be approved by the insurance company. This is very different from life insurance on humans where the policy pays a certain amount upon the death of the covered person. The difference between these types of policies is often a surprise to the horse owner who is unfamiliar with this distinction.

There are three common types of coverage for horses. The first type of policy specifies that the value of the horse be determined at the time of death. The owner has to prove the value of the horse or accept the appraiser's value. In the event the two cannot agree, some states have arbitration requirements.

The second type of policy requires that the owner prove the value of the horse every quarter.

And, the third type of policy has an agreeded-upon price. Often, the owners of the deceased horse think that they have this type of policy, when in fact, the value of the horse was never agreed upon. The predetermined or agreed-upon value policy may be best because, at a time when owners are grieving, the added burden of placing a value on the horse has already been done.

A common area of controversy involves cases where there was a failure to notify the insurer immediately of illness or surgery that was related to the horse's cause of death. When the insurance company is successful in showing that the insured failed to give immediate notice, the coverage may then be voided.

The owner of the horse must take the responsibility to make sure that all of the paperwork is filled out completely. This means complete the application, have the vet exam the horse and complete the certificate, then mail the paperwork along with the check to the insurance agent. Mark your calendar to repeat this process again, usually in 11 months. If you have any special circumstances or questions, call your agent. You may receive a renewal notice in the mail to help remind you to repeat the process, however mistakes happen and things get lost in the mail, so take it upon yourself to make sure all things happen when they should. If a horse dies after an insurance policy is allowed to lapse, the coverage will be considered void.

When a horse is euthanized, disputes are common and often end up in court. Obviously, under any kind of life insurance a beneficiary cannot kill the covered party and collect under the policy. In equine mortality insurance situations, however, disagreements can arise as to whether a sick or injured horse should be euthanized. Although all disputes have not been resolved by this action, the American Association of Equine Practitioners has established and published guidelines and criteria to be followed in determining whether euthanasia is proper:

- Is the condition chronic and incurable? Has the horse a prognosis for life?
- Is the horse a hazard to itself and its handlers?
- Will the horse require constant pain-relieving medication for the rest of its life?

Disputes often arise over when notification of illness should be given to the insurance company. Courts have held that when notice of an illness is not given, the insured assumes the risk of death for that particular illness. The horse owner or his bailee (the one taking care of the horse for the owner) are often forced to make "judgment calls" on whether the insurance company should be notified of a particular condition or illness. If the horses are in the care of others, the caretakers should be advised of the requirements and conditions of the policies regarding notice of illness or injury. Requirements of written notice should also be strictly followed. If the bailee takes on added responsibility when caring such valuable horses, the stable owner may indeed want to charge a higher price to board insured animals.

Another version of the question of notification under difficult circumstances, is when a horse is in distress and in a remote location. While it is possible that a horse may become sick while in a distant area of a ranch or a hunting horse becomes ill while on a pack trip, there are steps one can take to help the insurance policy stay in effect. In today's world of advanced communication, the guide on the pack-trip probably has a cellular telephone and communication can be made sooner than expected. In the event the animal has to be euthanized without proper witness, an autopsy may be performed by a vet later. Common sense may dictate that the best solution is to keep unusually valuable horses at home.

Does the insurance company have to be notified every time the horse has the sniffles? This can present very real problems to horse owners and their agents.

The best advice in notification cases is to PLAY IT SAFE. Give notice of ALL cases and situations where there is even the slightest chance of a problem condition or illness. Insurance companies often have a toll free number manned around the clock. In the event the horse must be spared any further suffering, permission to euthanize is usually given within 20 to 30 minutes. At the very LEAST, give notice to the insurance company of the following conditions:

- Lacerations requiring sutures
- Lameness lasting over two (2) days
- Any conditions requiring surgery
- Any bone fractures
- Colic which continues three (3) to four (4) hours
- Fever accompanied by no appetite
- Some policies require the owner to notify the insurance company of any visit by a veterinarian and to use a vet when necessary.

Loss-of-use Insurance

The "loss-of-use" clause may be an extension of the mortality contract. It covers the owner in the event of an accident which renders the animal unusable for a specified purpose. This is common for horses which earn considerable income as a race horse or a grand-prix jumper. If an injury renders the horse unusable for such purposes, the owner may suffer loss of income, thus the loss-of-use clause protects the owner from this risk. The loss-of-use clause or policy will usually specify how the animal can be used. For example, a 14-year-old girl decides to use one of her father's broodmares in jumping competition and the mare becomes injured and is later destroyed. This policy may be void if it specifically covered a "broodmare."

Major Medical or Surgical Insurance

Major medical is usually considered superior to surgical as it pays most of the non-surgical costs, plus the surgical fees.

Another type of insurance gaining popularity is for surgery only. Surgical coverage is only available with full mortality and basic coverage. Both of the above mentioned types of coverage will pay for necessary, non-cosmetic surgery. Colic surgery, is an example of necessary surgery and will be covered after the deductible has been satisfied and up to the maximum claim allowed on the contract. The difference between the two policies is coverage of non-surgical costs.

These policies are also contracts which specify what will be covered or what may be excluded, and as mentioned above, they vary. This coverage may be in addition to the mortality policy or a loss of use policy. Like health insurance for humans, the policy usually covers medical costs minus the deduction and with certain financial limits. An example of policy limits is if the policy covers the full surgeon's fee, but only allows for 25% of the other costs involved in surgery. The policy may also specify that the surgery be performed in a vet clinic. Frequently, a horse that has undergone colic surgery is not eligible to be reinsured when the annual policy comes due, or may be banned from coverage for a certain number of months to ensure proper healing.

Farm & Ranch Liability Coverage

The coverage necessary to protect the owner of a farm or ranch is much different than the coverage provided by a regular homeowner'

s policy. The liability coverage will vary for almost everyone reading this book. It will also differ from state to state depending upon protective legislation enacted to limit lawsuits. (See the Chapter 8, Liability of Horsemen.) Also, be aware that if the state in which you reside has any legislation regarding liability of horsemen, it usually will NOT cover attorney's fees or the fees of expert witnesses to prove your defense in court. Also, some state statutes will not cover defective tack. Because certain expenses involved in proving that you or your horse were not liable for an accident, you will want the extra insurance coverage mentioned in this section.

When selecting this type of coverage, review all activities which have ever been - or will ever be done on the property. For instance, will there ever be small shows where competition liability should be considered or a spectator could be injured? Will there be any guest trainers working there? Before changing the day-to-day operations, make sure the new changes will be covered. And, unfortunately, activities like horseback riding are considered "high-risk" and have seen great leaps in policy costs over the years. Ten years ago in 1983, a policy could be written for a livery stable for about $600. This livery stable could further be defined as one which owns 20 horses and rents them to the public to ride, boards about 20 horses and gives a few lessons. Today in 1993, the average premium for this same outfit would be about $3,500.

The Coverage of Actual Property

This additional coverage includes the outbuildings, barns, tack, machinery and feed. Most homeowner's policies do not cover items like tack. These items are considered restricted under the policy because not every homeowner would have such items. Your tack may not be covered if it is kept at a second location, i.e. the boarding stable or in your trailer. Also, don't expect the owner of the boarding stable to have coverage on <u>your</u> tack, after all his policy does not consider that he has an insurable interest in your tack. Ask your agent if your policy specifically endorses the second premises in which your property resides. Also, not covered, will be the silver on the saddles, unless you have an extension for precious metals.

Many times property is stolen while you are at a horse show or otherwise away from home. Note here that some theft policies require that the owner prove forced entry. In this case, you may want to get an added endorsement for an unlocked vehicle.

One of the strongest recommendations made by insurance agents today is to have photos or a video tape of your belongings and list the value of each item. This type of verification is only valid if you have two copies made of the tape or photos and send one to the insurance agent. If you only have one video tape of your belongings, it could be lost in a fire or difficult to prove it was indeed your possessions after they are all lost. Most insurance agents will provide guidelines and/or room by room accounting forms to help you take inventory of your property.

By now, you have realized that having enough insurance can be a substantial investment and before you invest in coverage, you may want to reevaluate your specific needs. Divide your belongings into three different categories. The first will be things you would find impossible to replace. These "catastrophic" losses would include your home, family, barn and horses. These you must find the resources to have insured. The second category will be items which could be replaced for a price. You will have to set your own limits of what price you are able to pay to have the items replaced. By selecting a number like $5,000, you are able to set your own limits and insure everything worth more than this amount. Once you set an amount - stick to it. The third category will be items that you could replace without any great hardship. Items under $5,000 are replaceable. This will help you keep your insurance costs down, while covering those items which really should be covered.

Auto Insurance and Coverage for Drivers

There are different types of coverage for different types of drivers. Not every driver is over 30, has a good record and pulls only a small two-horse trailer. Many drivers will fall into one of the other three categories: 1. high risk, 2. commercial license required, 3. hauling hazardous materials.

High risk drivers may have had accidents, tickets or other situations which restrict their coverage. This driver may be able to get coverage while hauling a horse trailer, but with limitations. The policy may not cover the trailer while not hooked-up to the truck, or the contents (like horses and tack). Or, it may be limited on it's liability coverage.

The second type of driver may be driving a larger rig. That is a truck and trailer weighing over 26,000 pounds. (The specifics of Interstate Trucking Laws are covered in Chapter Twelve beginning on page 91.)

The third type of driver is the one hauling hazardous materials. Farmers working with pesticides and fertilizers are frequently exposed to what can be defined as "hazardous materials." "I don't see how this would concern me?" you may say. Since hay is extremely flammable, it is considered hazardous material. Let your insurance agent know exactly what your needs are and be honest with them when they ask you questions.

Barn Safety Tips

After taking inventory of your barn and all of its possessions, you will want to take special precautions regarding safety. The following list will help make your barn a safer place.

- No Smoking signs should be posted and enforced.
- Fire extinguisher should be located near the electrical panel box, doors, feed and tack rooms.

- Fire exits should be clearly marked.
- Portable heaters are not recommended for barn use. Check with a plumbing and heating professional for safe alternatives.
- Make sure electrical outlets, light fixtures and wiring are safe. Have them checked every few years or whenever wear is noticed.
- Each stall should have vital information on the stall card along with a list of important phone numbers near the phone or office.
- First aid kits should be on hand, where everyone knows where they are.
- Keep all alleyways and traffic patterns clear in case of fire or other emergencies.
- Hay and bedding should be stored away from heat and electrical sources and, if possible, in a metal shed separate from the barn.

Check with your insurance agent and/or your state Cooperative Extension Service for more information about barn safety.

In addition to the selection of a suitable insurance policy, an emergency plan should be created, posted, and understood by all the adults and children.

Emergency Plan

Every good safety plan should include a list of emergency procedures. This plan could be viewed as an employee handbook, outlining the barn safety tips, an emergency plan, and procedures for safe learning and riding. Many first-time lessons cover safety techniques before being allowed to ride. Another good safety measure is for the riding instructor to have a current first aid card and know CPR.

The following are some suggestions for your emergency plan:

1. Call 911 if anyone is hurt. Have fire, police, sheriff, veterinarians or other information posted by the phone.

2. Contact the vet in the event a horse is injured.

3. Just as you would in an auto accident, get the insurance information from anyone involved and if there are witnesses, get their names and phone numbers.

4. Contact your insurance agent and have your insurance policy number handy.

5. Photos help answer questions for the insurance agent or adjuster. These photos may be of defective tack, the situation after an accident, injuries sustained, etc.

Finally, the horse owner should feel comfortable that his insurance agent knows his or her particular needs and is knowledgeable about all equine-related insurance.

Special Thanks to Carl Weil

Special thanks to Carl Weil, CIC. Carl Weil Insurance Company specializes exclusively in horse-related and outdoor activities coverage. His expertise in the field of equine insurance has led him to work as a consultant, helping owners of facilities manage their risks, thus becoming safer. As a result, the owner is eligible for better and more affordable insurance coverage. Weil also markets policies with safety standards for the horse industry. An example of a standard set forth in an insurance contract may be for riding instructor/trainer to comply with the following rule: All students must be at least six years old and wear boots and ASTM 1163 approved riding helmets complete with full harness-chin strap. This same standard may required the instructor to cover emergency procedures and tack safety during the first lesson.

Chapter 15

How to Select an Attorney

How to select an attorney who is capable and competent to represent a horse owner or an equine business, is a rather hard question to answer. As we all know, there is no shortage of lawyers and very little control or regulation of their advertising. In only a very few states are lawyers certified as being specialists in certain fields. No state certifies attorneys as being experts in equine law.

Few non-lawyers know that there are lists of attorneys available that give the education, background and experience of the attorney's listed. The oldest and most highly regarded list is a multi-volume work called "*Martindale Hubbell Law Directory*." This work makes an effort to always be current. *Martindale Hubbell* is published each year and covers the United States and aspires to list lawyers throughout the world. The most interesting feature of these books is the system used to rate lawyers. Although no rating system is able to rate the ability and integrity of each attorney perfectly, this system is based on the concept of "peer review." Lawyers who are already established and rated are asked to rate other lawyers who they know regarding their integrity and ability.

The first question asked of the rating of an attorney is regarding the candidate's integrity. Unless the rater can give a "very high" mark to integrity, the rating process goes no further. Once a "very high" or "v" rating is given to the candidate, the rater then considers his or her ability as an attorney. A range of "a" for excellent, or "b" for very good, and "c" for good are the options available to the rater. If the rater does not know enough about the candidate's ability as an attorney, or feels that, at least a good rating is not warranted, no rating is given. The highest rating that an attorney can receive is "av" or excellent ability and very high integrity. The majority of attorneys are not rated for a number of reasons, including the common one of simply not being known to the attorneys who have been asked to rate them. The "Martindale Hubbell" system is not perfect, but it at least gives some indication of the professional standing of particular lawyers.

In addition to the ratings of ability and integrity, some lawyers choose to pay for biographical listings in "Martindale Hubbell. The listings include the types of law practiced by the attorney and, if they so choose, a representative list of their clients. This biography is often very helpful in selecting lawyers for representation in specific areas of the law. However, the listed lawyer furnishes the copy and there is no independent verification of the accuracy of the information.

One problem with using *Martindale Hubbell* as a resource in finding a lawyer is its availability to non-lawyers. Sometimes it is carried in public libraries, but it is most commonly purchased and used by lawyers. Thus, the non-attorney might have some difficulty in finding *Martindale Hubbell* for their own use.

There are other law lists available, including some computer listings of attorneys and law firms. Availability of these lists is also a problem for the general public. They are created for and used principally by lawyers.

As mentioned above, there is very little, if any, regulation of advertising by lawyers. Bar associations and regulatory bodies have tried to set standards for attorney advertising. Misrepresentation and bad taste are hard to regulate. Because the purpose of advertising is to get business, advertisements are not the most accurate or reliable source for selecting an attorney.

When looking for an attorney with some background in equine-law, what is then the best source? Horse-related telephone directories may provide a beginning along with references and "word-of-mouth" recommendations. Receiving a recommendation of an attorney from a satisfied client should carry some weight during the decision making process. When a lawyer has withstood the test of fire with the client, and the client is satisfied with the representation, a recommendation from the client is worthy of serious consideration.

Most state and some local Bar Associations maintain a free lawyer referral service. Usually an advertisement of this service appears in the yellow pages. The names of attorneys with experience in the general area requested will be released to the caller. Each attorney on the list should be called and questioned regarding their experience in the particular area needed, their fees, etc. Some attorneys are prepared for this line of questioning and have prepared a letter or brochure answering frequently asked questions. Before selecting an attorney research, is the best policy.

Another little known source of referral for an attorney is from other attorneys practicing in the area. Referrals from other attorneys are also a possibility.

Even prosperous business people may ask, "Why is it important to have an attorney?" All business people, at some time, need the assistance of a qualified attorney. Having a good attorney on your team is as important as having a qualified accountant and a trusted veterinarian. The lawyer's role is to advise his or her clients; to counsel and aid them in their business planning; assist with the structure of the client's business; and work to avoid legal pitfalls.

Attorney's Fees

There are several ways in which an attorney may bill a client. The manner in which a client is charged varies depending on the type of case and the lawyer. Hourly rates are frequently used and vary greatly. Always ask the estimated hours needed in advance. Attorneys will charge for everything they do, including writing letters, meeting with you, research or phone calls. Other fees, such as filing fees, travel expenses, etc., may be added onto the hourly fee.

A **Flat Fee** may be appropriate for certain types of work. A simple will, for example, may cost a flat fee of $150. Again, flat fees are also subject to costs and expenses so ask ahead of time.

Retainer Fees are when a corporation or individual "retains" a lawyer for future use, usually on an annual basis. This fee is usually applied to the total at the end of the year.

Contingent Fees are not that common in the horse industry since they apply mainly to personal injury cases. This is when the attorney requests a percentage of the settlement.

Probably the most important role of the lawyer is to practice preventative law. That is, to get the client to come to the lawyer before there is a problem, before signing a contract, before changing business structures, before taking a bank loan to buy new stock or equipment, and before doing any other activity that could end in legal controversy. In other words, the lawyer's role in the horse business is to shut the barn door BEFORE the horse is stolen.

Glossary

A

Acceptance - In contract law, the offeree's notification to the offeror that the offeree agrees to be bound by the terms of a proposal.

Affirmative action - Job-hiring policies that give special consideration to minority groups.

Agent - A person authorized by another to act for or in place of him or her.

Agreement - A meeting of two or more minds. Often used as a synonym for contract.

Arbitration - The settling of a dispute by submitting it to a disinterested third party for decision.

Articles of partnership - A written agreement that sets forth each partner's rights in, and obligations to, the partnership.

Assumption of risk - A doctrine whereby a plaintiff may not recover for injuries or damages suffered from the inherent risks of equine sports.

Award - As a noun, not a trophy or ribbon, defines the amount of money, settlement or decision given to an injured party in a judicial proceeding.

B

Bailee - The person charged with the responsibility of caring for another's personal property. The individual who entrusts their property or animals to another is then called a Bailor. The agreement between these two becomes the Bailment.

Binder - A written, temporary insurance policy. Also, an extension of a current policy.

Business tort - Wrongful interference with the business or contractual relationships of others and unfair competition.

C

Condition - A qualification, provision, or clause in a contractual agreement, the occurrence of which creates, suspends, or terminates the obligations of the contracting parties.

Consignment - A transaction in which an owner of goods (the consignor) entrusts goods to be sold.

Contract - A set of promises constituting an agreement between parties, giving each a legal duty to the other and also the right to seek a remedy in the event of a breach of contract/broken promise.

Corporation - A legal entity created under the authority of the laws of a state or the federal government.

D

Debtor - A person who owes a sum of money or other obligations to another.

Dissolution - The formal disbanding of a partnership or corporation. It can take place by (1) agreement of the parties or the shareholders and board of directors, (2) by the death of a partner, (3) by the expiration of a time period stated in the agreement, (4) or by court order.

Dividend - A distribution to corporate shareholders, disbursed in proportion to the number of shares held.

E

Employment discrimination - Treating employees or job applicants unequally on the basis of race, sex, nationality, religion, or age; prohibited by Title VII of the Civil Rights Act of 1964 as amended.

Entrepreneur - One who initiates and assumes the financial risks of a new enterprise and manages the undertaking.

Estate - Everything a person owns, including animals, real estate, tack, jewelry ... everything.

Executor (Executrix) - The person responsible for administering a will.

Express contract - A contract, either oral or written. This varies from the implied contract.

Express warranty - An express warranty can be either orally or written specifically stating what an animal or product can do.

G

General partner - In a limited partnership, a partner who assumes responsibility for the management of the partnership and liability for all partnership debts.

Good faith purchaser - A purchaser who buys without notice of any circumstance that would put a person of ordinary prudence on inquiry as to whether the seller has valid ownership or title to the horse or property being sold.

Grandfather clause - A phrase used when zoning property to mean that when the property is sold it must then be used as the zoning requires. Often times when horse property is sold the new owner will not be able to have a horse on the property because of prior zoning laws.

H

Homestead exemption - A law allowing an owner to designate his or her house and adjoining land as a homestead and thus exempt it from liability for general debts.

I

Implied warranty - A warranty that the law implies either through the situation of the parties or the nature of the transaction.

Insurance - A contract in which, for a price the insurer can be reimbursed for loss, medical costs or liability costs.

Intestate - One who dies without having created a valid will.

J

Joint Tenancy - Ownership between two or more individuals. Upon the death of one of the joint tenants, his or her interest automatically passes to the others and cannot be transferred by the will of the deceased.

Jurisdiction - The authority of a court to hear and decide a specific action.

L

Law - A body of rules of conduct with legal force and effect.

Lease - A transfer by the lessor to a lessee for a period of time for consideration (usually payment). Upon termination of the lease, the property reverts to the lessor.

Lien - An encumbrance placed upon property to satisfy or protect a claim for payment of a debt.

Limited partnership - A partnership consisting of one or more general partners, who manage the business and are liable to the full extent of their personal assets for debts of the partnership; and of one or more limited partners, who contribute only assets and are liable only up to the amount contributed by them.

N

Negligence - The failure to exercise the standard of care that a reasonable person would exercise in similar circumstances.

O

Offer - An offeror's proposal to do something, which creates in the offeree accepting the offer a legal power to bind the offeror to the terms of the proposal by accepting the offer.

Offeree - A person to whom an offer is made.

Offeror - A person who makes an offer.

P

Partnership - An association of two or more persons involved in a business, usually for profit.

Performance - In contract law, the fulfillment of one's duties arising under a contract with another.

Personal property - Property that is movable; any property that is not real property.

Power of attorney - A document or instrument authorizing another to act as one's agent or attorney.

Precedent - A court decision that furnishes an example or authority for deciding subsequent cases in which identical or similar facts are presented.

Probate court - A court having jurisdiction over proceedings concerning the settlement of a person's estate.

Promissory note - A written instrument signed by a maker unconditionally promising to pay a certain sum of money to a payee or a holder on demand or on a specified date.

R

Real Property - Property attached to land.

Release - The relinquishment, concession, or giving up of a right, claim, or privilege, by the person in whom it exists or to whom it accrues, to the person against whom it might have been enforced or demanded.

Risk management - Planning that is undertaken to protect the insured's interest and to lower insurance premiums.

S

Sale - The passing of title to property from the seller to the buyer for a price.

Sales contract - A contract by means of which the ownership of goods is transferred from a seller to a buyer for a fixed price.

S Corporation - A form of business which has met certain requirements as set out by the Internal Revenue Code, that qualifies for special income-tax treatment. Essentially, an S corporation is taxed the same as a partnership, but its owners enjoy the privilege of limited liability.

Small claims courts - Special courts in which parties may litigate small claims (usually, claims involving $2,500 or less) Attorneys are not required in small claims courts, and in some states attorneys are not allowed to represent the parties.

Sole proprietorship - A business organization in which all of the firm's assets are owned by one individual. The owner, or sole proprietor, is entitled to all profits earned by the business and is personally liable for any losses or other obligations of the firm.

Strict liability - Liability regardless of fault. In tort law, strict liability is imposed on a merchant who introduces into commerce a good that is reasonably dangerous when in a defective condition.

T

Tort - In civil law, when wrongs arise from a breach of contract.

V

Valid contract - A properly constituted contract having legal strength or force.

W

Waiver - An intentional, knowing relinquishment of a legal right.

Warranty - An express warranty is included either written or orally usually in reference to the performance of goods sold. An implied warranty would be the general assumption that a horse has four legs, a head and a tail and reasonably fit.

Will - An instrument directing what is to be done with the testator's property upon his or her death, made by the property owner and revocable during his or her lifetime.

Index

Order Form

Did you borrow this book? Need a copy of your own?

Do you want information about marketing your products or services in the horse industry?

Do you want to get the job of your dreams?

Get down to business with business books for the horse industry from Pica Publishing.

Quantity	Title	Unit Price	Total
_____	**In The Balance** The Horseman's Guide to Legal Issues	$17.95	_____
_____	**Equi-Marketing** Marketing Principals Effectively Applied to the Horse Industry	$14.95	_____
_____	**Job Search Guide** Merchandising Yourself in a Tough Job Market	$7.00	_____

Shipping: ($2 first book, $1 each add'l): . . ______

Sales Tax: (Colorado residents add 6%): . . . ______

Canadian orders please add $4: . . . . ______

International orders add $5 for shipping: ______

Total: . . . . _____

U.S. checks or money orders only please. Allow 30 days for delivery. Mail this order form along with your check or money orders to:

Pica Publishing
28546 Golden Gate Canyon Road
Golden, CO 80403
or use the handy order line:
1-800-279-2001 Ext. 209